T0167766

Getting to Yes with China in Cyberspace

Scott Warren Harold, Martin C. Libicki, Astrid Stuth Cevallos

Prepared for RAND Internal Research & Development

For more information on this publication, visit www.rand.org/t/rr1335

Library of Congress Cataloging-in-Publication Data
ISBN: 978-0-8330-9249-6

Published by the RAND Corporation, Santa Monica, Calif.
© Copyright 2016 RAND Corporation
RAND® is a registered trademark

Cover Image: US President Barack Obama (R) checks hands with Chinese president Xi Jinping after a press conference in the Rose Garden of the White House September 25, 2015 in Washington, DC. President Obama is welcoming President Jinping during a state arrival ceremony. Photo by Olivier Douliery/ABACA (Sipa via AP Images).

Support RAND
Make a tax-deductible charitable contribution at
www.rand.org/giving/contribute

www.rand.org

Preface

Since the founding of the People's Republic of China in 1949, the U.S.-China relationship has been characterized by substantial areas of conflict, confrontation, and strategic mistrust. The tensions that divide the two countries have been growing in importance in recent years. Unfortunately, they apply just as much to cyberspace as to relations in the physical world. Indeed, of all the areas where the relationship between the two sides is troubled, cyberspace has been one of the most contentious. The United States and China began formal negotiations in 2013 to resolve such differences, only to see them abruptly end in 2014, when China broke them off in response to the U.S. indictment of several Chinese military officers on charges related to cyber-espionage activities.

This report is a response to the absence of a formal dialogue and explores U.S. policy options for managing relations with China over this critical policy area. It looks at two basic questions: Can the United States and China return to meaningful formal negotiations over norms and rules in cyberspace? And, if so, what areas are most likely to yield agreement, and what might be exchanged for what?

This analysis should be of interest to two communities: those concerned with U.S. relations with China and those concerned with developing norms of conduct in cyberspace, notably those that enhance security and freedom.

Funding for this report was provided, in part, by donors and by the independent research and development provisions of the RAND Corporation's contracts for the operation of its U.S. Department of Defense federally funded research and development centers.

Contents

Summary

Since the People's Republic of China was founded in 1949, the U.S.-China relationship has been characterized by substantial areas of conflict, confrontation, and strategic mistrust. By mid-2015, many leading U.S. specialists on China described a rapid deterioration in bilateral ties, which could be described as an across-the-board contest; U.S. analysts now call for a new grand strategy toward China to balance its rising power. A growing number of Chinese observers similarly appear to see relations as reflecting a "silent contest" between the world's two most powerful countries.[1]

Unfortunately, this pattern of growing tensions applies just as much to cyberspace; indeed, cyberspace has become one of the most contentious arenas. By some accounts, tension in this area is one of the main sources of a broader deterioration in ties. However, while U.S. dissatisfaction with Chinese behavior in cyberspace plays a large role in how the United States views China overall, China's concerns about U.S. behavior in cyberspace play a substantially more modest role in shaping how China views the United States overall, which may help explain why the two sides have had limited success in sustaining dialogue over the issue to date. The United States and China initiated a formal bilateral dialogue on cyberspace in 2013, but the Chinese cut off this dialogue in 2014, after the United States indicted five People's Liberation Army officers for conducting cyber espionage against U.S.

---

[1] David Shambaugh, "Coping with a Conflicted China," *Washington Quarterly*, Vol. 34, No. 1, winter 2011, pp. 7–27; Jane Perlez, "Strident Video by Chinese Military Casts U.S. as Menace," *New York Times*, October 31, 2013; Edward Wong, "Chinese Colonel's Hard-Line Views Seep into the Mainstream," *New York Times*, October 3, 2015.

targets. While the bilateral Cyber Working Group appears to have been abandoned as an approach, discussions on cyberspace issues did occur at the bilateral Strategic and Economic Dialogue in summer 2015, and an initial agreement to move forward on the issue took center stage on the outcomes list of the Xi-Obama summit held in Washington in September 2015. Still, substantial questions persist about the two nations' relationship in cyberspace. In the absence of a set of fully fleshed-out norms and procedures to modulate troublesome activity and set rules for cyberspace, the issue will continue to represent a substantial risk to the bilateral relationship, regional peace and stability, and global order.

From the U.S. perspective, three issues dominate. The primary complaint has been with China's multiple and repeated intrusions into corporate networks to steal intellectual property and proprietary business information. A second concern has been the growing penetration of U.S. systems through cyberspace for traditional espionage purposes related to national security (e.g., the penetration of the Office of Personnel Management revealed in mid-2015, possibly for the purpose of compiling enormous databases on U.S. citizens [and also, potentially, their Chinese contacts] for potential recruitment or blackmail). A third U.S. concern is over the prospect that China might be prepared to use a cyberattack to take down U.S. critical infrastructure during a crisis. A fourth concern is the lack of clarity over each side's use of cyberattack in warfare and the risk in escalation.

For its part, China decries U.S. accusations of hacking and proclaims that it is itself a victim of cyberattacks coming from the United States. Chinese officials and commentators complain about U.S. restrictions on market access for Chinese telecommunications firms such as Huawei and ZTE Corporation. Chinese commentaries also bemoan U.S. funding of Internet censorship–circumvention technology and argue for the right of states to control the information that individuals can access within their boundaries (a notion known as *cyber sovereignty*). China observers also decry U.S. Internet "hegemony," noting that many of the routers and servers, as well as the software used to support the backbone of the Internet in China, are produced by and/or controlled by U.S. firms.

Given these divergent views, and in the aftermath of China's abandonment of formal talks on cybersecurity with the United States, we were drawn to and motivated by several urgent policy questions in writing this report. Can the United States and China return to meaningful formal negotiations over norms and rules in cyberspace? If so, can such discussions between the two countries lead to a common understanding about rules in cyberspace? What are the feasible paths to getting to useful agreements in cyberspace? And what areas are most likely to yield agreement, and what might be exchanged for what? In thinking about how to manage the critical challenge of U.S.-China relations in cyberspace, we conducted extensive research resulting in this report. Its primary contribution to the public policy debate over the U.S.-China relationship in cyberspace is threefold.

First, the report concisely scopes the issue for the reader, creating a single document that surveys the broad literature on this question and distills it to its critical elements.

Second, the report presents insights from interviews with leading Chinese and American cyberspace policy experts across the governments, militaries, think tanks, and academic communities of the two countries, thereby leveraging a previously unused methodology that allows the reader to hear Chinese and American concerns directly from leading thinkers on both sides.

And third, the report presents a novel set of conclusions, suggesting that, to gain Chinese agreement on desired targeting norms in cyberspace, the United States may need to simultaneously incentivize China to come to, and stay at, the bargaining table by raising the costs of refusing to negotiate over cybersecurity norms and incentivize what is offered.

We have concluded that, despite the apparent September 2015 agreement between U.S. President Barack Obama and Chinese President Xi Jinping, the two sides are likely to remain deeply divided over cyberspace unless they formally negotiate a more wide-ranging and robust set of agreements detailing terminology, metrics and standards of proof, and norms. At their core, China and the United States have very different perspectives on the development of cyberspace and on what each can ask each other. The two countries also have different perspectives on the roles played by norms and the legitimacy of state actions used to enforce such norms. This does not mean that agreement is impossible. China may accede to U.S. wishes as a way to relieve pressure from the United States, but it is unclear whether such agreements will survive beyond their short-term utility in helping China avoid sanctions (one possible interpretation of what led to the surprising September 2015 cyber agreement). The path to a lasting agreement would, in our opinion, require China to commit to and follow through on changing their behavior in cyberspace. To say that these are difficult or even unlikely does not imply that they are impossible. The following summary of our work explains how we reached these conclusions.

When it comes to laying the groundwork for understanding the two sides' positions on cybersecurity issues by describing two very different ways that countries can understand norms, power, and the role and interests of the state. We posit two ideal types. One is *Red deterrence*, which extracts from Chinese practice. The other is *Blue deterrence*, which extracts from U.S. practice. Countries that practice Red deterrence regard norms as a reflection of the underlying power balance and the interests of the state. They view the power relationships among countries as primary and their conduct vis-à-vis norms as secondary. Those that practice Blue deterrence view norms as more akin to neutral, mutually agreed-upon rules and boundaries that serve the common good of all the actors in the international system. They view norms that guide conduct of substantially greater importance and see the power relationships among states as less relevant to the need to ensure the enforcement of norms.

One example of the difference arising from adherence to each of the two ideal types: the United States sought to punish North Korea for its attack on Sony Pictures Entertainment to signal to all countries that cyberattacks cannot be conducted with impunity (e.g., a putative norm). China was reluctant to take actions against North Korea for this cyberattack, in part because the intrusion was a very minor issue in the scope of a more complex relationship with its difficult neighbor. The odds of a misunderstanding are likely to rise to the extent that the United States thinks China's behavior is cynical (when it favors power over rules), and China thinks that U.S. behavior is hypocritical (when it uses rules to mask power).

Understanding the potential pathways to successful negotiations to stabilize the cyber relationship between the United States and China requires understanding the essential issues between the two countries in cyberspace and their perspectives on these issues. There is a great deal of history between the two countries on the issue of cybersecurity, starting from Chinese intrusions into Department of Energy laboratories, government agencies, military postgraduate schools, and defense firms, as well as continuing to compromise networks of numerous corporations, with particular emphasis on media firms and those doing business in China. Chinese complaints tend to be less specific: They focus on U.S. hegemony in cyberspace, notably through the success of U.S. software firms and its dominance of Internet routing and governance institutions. Less discussed in public are U.S. intrusion sets in Chinese systems, an issue highlighted by the allegations made by former U.S. National Security Administration contractor Edward Snowden. Chinese officials also bridle at U.S. complaints, not only about Chinese intrusions but over Chinese suppression of Internet freedom. The report draws on our review of the relevant Western secondary-source literature and our analyses of Chinese writings on cybersecurity, as well as the results of past attempts to make progress on cybersecurity through the Track Two dialogues among the Center for Strategic and International Studies, the Chinese Institutes of Contemporary International Relations, and the official U.S.-China Cyber Working Group.

Additionally, in May 2015, we conducted a set of interviews with Chinese respondents and high-level interlocutors. In some cases, we report directly on what we heard. In other cases, we use the material to consider alternative negotiating approaches (e.g., bilateral versus multilateral, synchronous versus asynchronous) and postures. The primary insights follow.

Formally, the Chinese remain adamant that they cannot negotiate while People's Liberation Army officers are under indictment—but they are open to less-than-formal discussions and in many cases, proposed potential workarounds. One high-level interlocutor even suggested that "China is not willing to let a single issue obstruct the broader relationship."[2] This implies that a workaround for China's refusal to negotiate might exist, something that may help explain President Xi's offer to accept U.S. formulations on norms targeting cyberspace during the September 2015 summit meeting.

The Chinese we talked to rarely bothered to make even a *pro forma* denial that China conducts cyber espionage in general or economically motivated cyber espionage in particular.

Chinese interviewees believe that the United States has militarized cyberspace—and they are determined not to be left too far behind in what they view as a competition (albeit one they regret taking place).

The Chinese see cybersecurity talks as a way to appease U.S. irritation more than to achieve anything specific. In contrast, the United States places a much higher emphasis on using such dialogues to resolve cybersecurity issues.

The Chinese do not appear to have a well-formed set of demands—not even a diminution of U.S. cyber espionage—that they would be willing to trade for any significant cessation of economically motivated cyber espionage (much less all categories of cyber espionage). Thus, it is difficult to see such cyber espionage as falling within the cyber trade space.

The Chinese do not accept the U.S. proposition that a country has a right to unilaterally respond to cyberattacks *qua* the Law of Armed Conflict.

One idea we mooted was for both countries to abjure attacks on each other's critical infrastructure. There was considerable receptivity to this proposal, even when coupled with the proviso that both sides would *also* have to abjure cyber espionage on such targets. The sticking point was attribution. The United States believes it can catch China cheating and would like some process by which cheating, once discovered, is acknowledged so that some consequences (other than merely reputational ones) would follow. China believes it cannot catch the cheating by the United States and is apprehensive of any agreement that would put them at a corresponding disadvantage. Thus, any serious agreement would need a process that both sides could trust and/or

---

2   Interview with high-level Chinese interlocutor, Beijing, May 2015.

some way to increase China's confidence it is own attribution capabilities. This is a very difficult challenge but not, in our opinion, an absolutely hopeless one, provided that both sides were to agree to work on it in good faith. Were the United States and China to do so, we provide an initial set of thoughts that could be explored about how to move forward in this area. It is not clear, however, that China wants to get to yes on the issue—i.e., truly resolve it by establishing mutually agreed-upon and respected norms with respect to targeting in cyberspace—so much as it wants simply to get away from the issue. If that assessment is correct, then the United States is not likely to see its recently negotiated agreement with China on cyberspace lead to lasting changes in Chinese actions in cyberspace.

Abbreviations

CBM	confidence-building measures
CICIR	Chinese Institutes of Contemporary International Relations
CPC	Communist Party of China
CSIS	Center for Strategic and International Studies
DoD	U.S. Department of Defense
EMCE	economically motivated cyber espionage
ICANN	Internet Corporation for Assigned Names and Numbers
IP	Internet Protocol
ITU	International Telecommunications Union
LOAC	Law of Armed Conflict
NSA	National Security Agency
OPM	Office of Personnel Management
PLA	People's Liberation Army
PRC	People's Republic of China
S&ED	Strategic and Economic Dialogue
SCO	Shanghai Cooperation Organization
TRIPS	Trade-Related Aspects of Intellectual Property Rights
UN	United Nations
USCYBERCOM	U.S. Cyber Command

CHAPTER ONE

The "Cyber Problem" in U.S.-China Relations

Since the founding of the People's Republic of China (PRC) in 1949, the U.S.-China relationship has been characterized by substantial areas of conflict, confrontation, and strategic mistrust. The tensions that divide the two sides have been growing in importance in recent years, as one study by a pair of leading experts from both the United States and China has noted.[1] Indeed, by mid-2015, many leading U.S. specialists on China described a rapid deterioration in bilateral ties, with one referring to the U.S.-China relationship as having passed a "tipping point," another warning that "an across-the-board contest now dominates U.S.-China relations," and a pair of respected former government officials calling for "revising U.S. grand strategy toward China" so as to better balance the latter's rising power.[2]

China similarly sees relations with the United States as deeply troubled and points to the U.S. rebalance to the Asia-Pacific region

---

[1] Kenneth N. Lieberthal and Wang Jisi, *Addressing U.S.-China Strategic Distrust*, Washington, D.C.: The John L. Thornton China Center, Brookings Institution, 2012. See also Jon Lindsay, Tai Ming Cheung, and Derek Reveron's comprehensive study of U.S.-Chinese relationships in cyberspace: Jon R. Lindsay, Tai Ming Cheung, and Derek Reveron, *China and Cybersecurity: Espionage, Strategy, and Politics in the Digital Domain*, Oxford: Oxford University Press, 2015.

[2] David M. Lampton, "A Tipping Point in US-China Relations Is Upon Us," *US-China Perception Monitor*, May 11, 2015; David Shambaugh, "In a Fundamental Shift, China and the US Are Now Engaged in All-Out Competition," *South China Morning Post*, June 14, 2015; Robert D. Blackwill and Ashley J. Tellis, *Revising U.S. Grand Strategy Toward China*, Washington, D.C.: Council on Foreign Relations, Council Special Report No. 72, May 2015.

as "worse than containment," arguing that the trouble China has had with its neighbors in recent years stems from U.S. efforts to embolden and/or manipulate regional actors into adopting a posture of confrontation with Beijing.[3] Indeed, Chinese leaders have appeared to be surprised that regional actors continue to welcome the United States, having anticipated that China's growing economic weight would naturally lead to the withering away of the U.S.-focused alliance system.[4] U.S. efforts to support Japan over the Senkaku Islands, and U.S. calls to freeze construction in the South China Sea while continuing to engage in freedom of navigation exercises, also cause alarm in China. And continued U.S. support for global human-rights norms and criticism of China's failure to meet these international standards of civilized behavior are seen as a threat to the regime that could conceivably lead to a "color revolution" that might topple the Communist Party of China (CPC).

Unfortunately, this pattern of growing tensions about relations as seen from both sides in the physical world applies just as much to cyberspace. Indeed, of the areas in which the relationship between the two countries is troubled, cyberspace has been one of the most contentious. While the two sides initiated a formal bilateral dialogue on cyberspace in 2013, the talks were cut off by China in 2014. The absence of firm commitments to norms governing activity in this new domain and setting the rules of the road for cyberspace also represents a substantial risk for the bilateral relationship, regional peace and stability, and global order.

This report is a response to the absence of a formal dialogue and explores U.S. policy options for managing relations with China over this critical policy area. It looks at two basic questions: Can the United States and China return to meaningful formal negotiations over norms

---

[3] Lyle J. Goldstein, "How China Sees America's Moves in Asia: Worse than Containment," *National Interest*, October 29, 2014; Andrew J. Nathan and Andrew Scobell, "How China Sees America: The Sum of Beijing's Fears," *Foreign Affairs*, September/October 2012.

[4] Jae Ho Chung, "China's Evolving Views of the Korean-American Alliance, 1953–2012," *Journal of Contemporary China*, Vol. 23, No. 87, pp. 425–442.

and rules in cyberspace? And if so, what areas are most likely to yield agreement and what might be exchanged for what?

In a previous generation, when nuclear weapons atop intercontinental ballistic missiles guided by space-based overhead reconnaissance and targeting architectures were coming into being, U.S. experts rarely had an opportunity to engage directly with their Soviet counterparts to understand how they defined the problems associated with deterrence, their thinking about global norms, their assessments of how to communicate signals, or their insights into how best to approach cooperation and de-escalation. While the parallels between cyber and nuclear issues are often exaggerated and inexact, one area of commonality is in the fact that perceptions of vulnerability in both arenas have had and are continuing to have a substantial negative impact on bilateral stability between leading world powers. Fortunately, unlike in the Cold War, researchers in the United States and China can and regularly do exchange views on important issues of the day, creating the prospect for greater understanding and more accurate mutual assessments of the security challenges associated with managing their bilateral relationship.

Despite these opportunities for information exchanges about cybersecurity, the prospects of cooperation over cyberspace have not been promising to date. To provide (but not necessarily endorse) two approaches toward cooperation, we note that Karl Rauscher and Yonglin Zhou of the EastWest Institute have proposed "fighting spam to build trust," while Kenneth Lieberthal and Peter W. Singer of the Brookings Institution have proposed an entire set of cooperative measures.[5]

In the years since these studies were published, however, the relations between the two countries have only worsened over the cyber issue. As China cyber specialist Amy Chang argued, "the two nations continue to face substantial obstacles in developing cooperative efforts and improving mutual understanding" on the issue of cyberspace, to

---

[5] Karl Frederick Rauscher and Zhou Yonglin, *Fighting Spam to Build Trust*, New York: EastWest Institute, 2011; Kenneth Lieberthal and Peter W. Singer, *Cybersecurity and U.S.-China Relations*, Washington, D.C.: 21st Century Defense Initiative, The John L. Thornton China Center, Brookings Institution, February 2012.

the point that "relations have devolved to near-complete distrust of each other's motives, actions, and agendas, affecting other facets of the bilateral relationship." Chang further points out that

> China's network security policies are motivated . . . by the Chinese Communist Party's goal of maintaining its own governing power . . . [by ensuring] domestic stability, territorial integrity, modernization, and economic growth, while simultaneously preparing for the possibility of militarized cyber conflict in the future.[6]

Similarly, cyber specialist James Lewis has noted that "political differences, competition for regional influence, and a general desire to undermine the U.S. position in Asia" are characteristic of Chinese policy toward cybersecurity, and these hamper the prospects of U.S.-China cooperation.[7] Chang agrees, noting that "there currently exist few incentives for China to cooperate meaningfully with more developed nations on curbing intellectual property theft [or] cybercrime."[8]

While many U.S. specialists see few prospects for substantial cooperation in the near term, a number of Chinese observers—officials and think-tank experts and scholars—have recognized the importance of finding a path forward on this issue, either through bilateral negotiations, multilateral agreements, or both. For example, the Chinese government's proposed "International Code of Conduct for Information Security," submitted to the United Nations (UN) in February 2014, notes the absence of "comprehensive 'traffic rules'" and speaks of the desirability of an "open and sustained process of building international consensus" over cyberspace issues.[9] Similarly, in a speech in Washington, D.C., in December 2014, Ma Xinming, the deputy director-gen-

---

[6] Amy Chang, *Warring State: China's Cybersecurity Strategy*, Washington, D.C.: Center for a New American Security, December 2015, pp. 7 and 10.

[7] Julia Oh, "Cyber Cooperation in Northeast Asia: An Interview with James Lewis," National Bureau of Asian Research, Policy Q&A, March 17, 2015.

[8] Chang, 2015, p. 22.

[9] "An International Code of Conduct for Information Security—China's Perspective on Building a Peaceful, Secure, Open and Cooperative Cyberspace," statement prepared for a

eral of the Treaty and Laws Department at the Ministry of Foreign Affairs of China, argued that the United States and China need to work together to "help establish [the] fundamental order and rules of cyberspace" and put forth a Chinese proposal for employing the UN charter to "define the fundamental principles of cyber activities."[10] And the official English-language *China Daily* has published numerous articles in recent years, many based on interviews with Chinese officials and think-tank analysts, that seek to convey the reassuring message that China is "open to cybersecurity teamwork."[11]

Chinese academic scholars, such as Shen Yi of Fudan University, have echoed these views, arguing that the two sides need to reach an "agreement on some clear behavioral regulations and norms for cyberspace to cut down on the negative impact of uncertainty."[12] Likewise, Dong Qingling, a professor at the University of International Business and Economics in Beijing, has argued that "it is becoming increasingly urgent for China and the United States to regulate conflicts and build confidence in cyberspace."[13] This may be because, as Yi Wenli, an assistant researcher at the National Information Technology Research Center, argues, the increasing suspicion and distrust on both sides of the Pacific are reducing the room for dialogue on cybersecurity issues,

---

conference in Geneva hosted by the UN Institute for Disarmament Research, February 10, 2014.

[10] Ma Xinming, "What Kind of Internet Order Do We Need?" *Chinese Journal of International Law*, Vol. 14, No. 2, 2015, pp. 399–403.

[11] See, for example, Wang Xu, "China 'Open to' Cybersecurity Teamwork," *China Daily*, September 18, 2015.

[12] Shen Yi, "Responding to the Challenge of the 'Offensive Internet Freedom Strategy': Analyzing Sino-US Competition and Cooperation in Global Cyberspace," ["Yingdui jingongxing hulianwang ziyou zhanlüe de tiaozhan: Xi Zhong-Mei zai quanqiu xinxi kongjian de jingzheng yu hezuo"], *World Economics and Politics* [*Shijie jingji yu zhengzhi*], No. 2, 2012, pp. 69–79.

[13] Dong Qingling, "Confidence-Building for Cybersecurity Between China and the United States," *China International Studies*, July/August 2014, pp. 57–68.

even in areas of common interest, meaning the window of opportunity to negotiate norms and rules could be closing.[14]

Formal and regular continuing and meaningful negotiations are clearly necessary if the two sides want to avoid allowing uncertainty and unwelcome activities in cyberspace to drive their relations in a negative direction. For policymakers on both sides of the Pacific, cybersecurity is a relatively new and quickly developing area where market- and national security–driven technological changes are erasing the strategic stability–reinforcing benefits of the distance that separates the United States and China. The two sides' disagreements over cyberspace tend to cluster around five areas: (1) the legitimacy of the use of cyberspace for economic or industrial espionage; (2) national security uses of cyberspace for more-traditional forms of espionage and intelligence gathering; (3) the prospective use of cyberspace for military operations; (4) the putative rights of states to control information access within their borders (referred to by China as *cyber sovereignty*); and (5) the issue of how international norms, rules, and the physical architecture of the Internet should be governed.

From the U.S. perspective, the primary complaint with China has been its multiple and repeated intrusions into corporate networks to steal intellectual property or proprietary business information. While the overall value of such theft is unknown, one observer, GEN (ret.) Keith Alexander,[15] former director of the National Security Agency (NSA), has estimated the cost of China's intellectual property theft from the United States at $300 billion a year.[16] After years of privately communicating its views to China that such intrusions were not a legit-

---

[14] Yi Wenli, "Divergence Between China and the U.S. and the Path Toward Cooperation in Cyberspace" ["Zhong-Mei zai Wangluo Kongjian de Fenqi yu Hezuo Lujing"], *Contemporary International Relations* [*Xiandai Guoji Guanxi*], Vol. 22, No. 4, July/August 2012, pp. 124–141.

[15] Jim Garamone, "Cybercom Chief Details Cyberspace Defense," American Forces Press Service, September 23, 2010.

[16] The Center for Strategic and International Studies (CSIS) estimates are roughly a tenth as much (see CSIS, *The Economic Impact of Cybercrime and Cyber Espionage*, July 2013), and a case can be made based on economic logic and the nature of economic development that the net harm to the United States may even lower than that.

imate use of its military and intelligence services with no notable effect, in 2014, the United States took the next step of indicting five serving officers in the People's Liberation Army (PLA) on hacking charges, a move that led China to suspend its participation in the U.S.-China Cyber Working Group.[17]

A second concern has been the growing penetration of U.S. systems through cyberspace for traditional espionage purposes related to national security. To date, U.S. administrations have not claimed that such activities violate any norms with respect to the appropriate use of cyberspace for espionage. However, the frequency and magnitude of a number of recently disclosed intrusions into U.S. computer systems, including, most notably, the June 2015 revelations about the hacking of the Office of Personnel Management (OPM), has led some commentators to begin talking about the need to clarify under what circumstances, if any, "the definition of what constitutes a 'cyberattack' might need to expand to include 'major disruptions' that nevertheless do not produce physical harm to the affected state."[18] Some observers have suggested that there are links between the intrusions into private-sector firms, such as health care provider Anthem, and attacks on U.S. government departments, such as OPM and the Department of Homeland Security (hacked in late 2014), possibly for the purpose of compiling enormous databases of U.S. civil servants and their China contacts or relatives for potential monitoring or recruitment.[19]

Separately, a third U.S. concern is over the prospect that China might be prepared to use a cyberattack to take down U.S. critical infrastructure during a crisis. The current NSA director, ADM Michael S.

---

[17] Michael S. Schmidt and David E. Sanger, "5 in China Army Face U.S. Charges of Cyberattacks," *New York Times*, May 19, 2014; Chen Weihua and Li Xiaokun, "China Demands Charges Be Dropped," *China Daily*, May 22, 2014.

[18] Ashley Deeks, "Tallinn 2.0 and a Chinese View of the Tallinn Process," *Lawfare* blog, May 31, 2015.

[19] Ellen Nakashima, "Security Firm Finds Link Between China and Anthem Hack," *Washington Post*, February 27, 2015a; Ellen Nakashima, "With Series of Major Hacks, China Builds Database on Americans," *Washington Post*, June 5, 2015c; Stephen Braun, "Official Says Hackers Hit Up to 25,000 Homeland Security Employees," *Washington Post*, August 23, 2014.

Rogers, has testified that China has compromised the U.S. power grid through intrusions that left behind software implants (often referred to as *back doors*) that could be used to wreak havoc in a crisis.[20] There are also concerns that the United States and China could misread each other's actions and signals in cyberspace during a crisis in ways that could lead to escalation. Due to the relatively opaque nature of cyberspace, it is also possible that the two sides could misattribute signals from each other or misattribute actions taken by a third party as coming from each other, especially if a malicious or self-interested actor were to route attacks on the other side through U.S. or Chinese servers during a particularly tense period in the bilateral relationship. The United States and China are concerned about how each side would use cyberattacks in warfare and the escalation risks that such use may entail.

Furthermore, the United States has expressed concerns over China's treatment of U.S. corporations under the guise of protecting its security.[21]

Finally, the United States has criticized China for suppressing free speech on the Internet. Patterns of behavior, such as the early 2015 incident in which packet-flooding (i.e., distributed denial of service) attacks disabled software-distribution site GitHub,[22] may become the subject of future U.S.-China negotiations.

For its part, China decries U.S. accusations of hacking and proclaims that it is itself a victim of cyberattacks coming from the United States. Chinese officials and commentators complain about U.S. restrictions on market access for Chinese telecommunications firms Huawei and ZTE. Chinese commentaries also bemoan U.S. funding of Internet censorship–circumvention technology and argue for the rights of states to govern what individuals can access within their boundaries

---

[20] Ken Dilanian, "NSA Director: China Can Damage US Power Grid," Associated Press, November 20, 2014.

[21] Paul Mozur, "New Rules in China Upset Western Tech Companies," *New York Times*, January 29, 2015. China has since postponed application of those rules.

[22] Nicole Perlroth, "China Is Said to Use Powerful New Weapon to Censor the Internet," *New York Times*, April 10, 2015; "China Behind Cyberattack on US Sites, Report Says," *San Francisco Chronicle*, May 8, 2015.

(known as *cyber sovereignty*). PRC observers complain bitterly about U.S. Internet "hegemony," noting that most of the routers and servers and the software used to support the backbone of Internet in China are produced by U.S. firms.[23] Others, such as Jiang Chong, director of the Economic Security Research Center at the China Institutes of Contemporary International Relations (CICIR), note the "monopolistic advantages" [*longduan youshi*] of the United States in such areas as technological standards, basic facilities, intellectual property resources, and domain name resolution, arguing that these constitute a form of "cyber dominance" [*wangluo zhudaoquan*] or even "cyber hegemony" [*wangluo baquan*].[24] And finally, many Chinese observers tend to argue that the Domain Name System used to create Internet websites, currently managed by the Internet Corporation for Assigned Names and Numbers (ICANN), should be transformed into an international organization, such as the UN (thereby giving China a voice in global Internet governance).[25]

Until recently, U.S. criticism of China has been mostly oblique, with veiled references to Chinese activity but not specifying China.[26]

---

[23] See, for example, Guo Ji, "Cyber Should Not Become a New Tool of American Hegemony: Starting from an Explanation of the 'PRISM-gate' Incident [Wangluo buying chengwei Meiguo baquan xin gongju: Cong 'Lingjingmen' shijian shuokai qu]," *Seeking Truth* [*Qiu Shi*], No. 15, 2013, pp. 57–59.

[24] Jiang Chong, "Cyber: The Invisible New Battlefront [Wangluo: Kanbujian de xin zhanxian]," *Seeking Truth* [*Qiu Shi*], No. 13, 2010, pp. 53–55.

[25] Yang Jian, "The Nature of the Contextual Contradictions in America's Use of the Phrase 'Cyberspace Global Commons' [Meiguo 'Wangluo kongjian quanqiu gongyu shuo' de yujing maodun jiqi benzhi]," *International Survey* [*Guoji guancha*], No. 1, 2013, pp. 46–52; Lu Chuanying, "An Attempt to Analyze the Current Global Governance Dilemma in Cyberspace [Shixi dangqian wangluo kongjian quanqiu zhili kunjing]," *Contemporary International Relations* [*Xiandai guoji guanxi*], No. 11, 2013, pp. 48–54; Jiang Li, Zhang Xiaolan, and Xu Feibiao, "The International Cybersecurity Dilemma and a Way Out [uoji wangluo anquan hezuo de kunjing yu chulu]," *Contemporary International Relations* [*Xiandai guoji guanxi*], No. 9, 2013, pp. 52–58. Yang and Lu are researchers at the Shanghai Institutes for International Studies; Jiang, Zhang, and Xu are researchers at the CICIR in Beijing.

[26] The primary exception was the January 2010 criticism of China over its treatment of Google: To wit, the intrusion of Chinese hackers into Google's network *and* China's censorship over Google content led Google to decamp from China to Hong Kong. Secretary of State Hillary Clinton criticized China's behavior toward Google in early 2010 and demanded

The early 2013 publication of the Mandiant report on a Chinese hacker group belonging to the PLA justified U.S. officials' public singling out China.[27] Several months later, the topic of Chinese cyber espionage highlighted the summit between President Barack Obama and President Xi Jinping (held at the Sunnylands estate in Rancho Mirage, California). The summit marked an upgrading of formal (i.e., Track One) discussions on cyber between the two countries. These negotiations indicated a willingness of the two countries to talk, but, with China denying that they carried out any cyber espionage activities, the results of the discussions were meager. Then, in May 2014, when the United States surprised China by indicting five PLA officers for carrying out cyber espionage, China responded by suspending the official Cyber Working Group negotiations. No further Cyber Working Group sessions were held, though the U.S. side raised the cyber issue with China during the summer 2015 Strategic and Economic Dialogue (S&ED) sessions. Then, immediately prior to the September 2015 China–U.S. summit, Meng Jianzhu, head of the CPC's Political and Legal Affairs Commission, visited the United States to coordinate cyber issues after leaks in the media suggested that the United States was planning to impose economic sanctions on Chinese firms, which would presumably have derailed the Xi-Obama summit.[28] In the aftermath of Meng's visit, to the surprise of many observers, the two sides announced an agreement at the summit on cybersecurity, which defined certain kinds of commercial espionage as off limits, with both parties vowing to increase bilateral cooperation. While this was a good first step, many

---

an explanation. See Cecilia Kang, "Hillary Clinton Calls for Web Freedom, Demands China Investigate Google Attack," Washington Post, January 22, 2010.

[27] Mandiant, *APT1: Exposing One of China's Cyber Espionage Units*, March 2013. Note that there had been direct discussion of Chinese espionage well before the report came out, such as during earlier Strategic and Economic Dialogues. And Secretary of State Clinton referred to China's hacking of Google in 2010.

[28] Eric Beech and Ben Blanchard, "U.S., Chinese Officials Meet on Cyber Security Issues: White House," Reuters, September 12, 2015.

analysts believe it will require substantial follow-through to be truly meaningful.[29]

Purpose and Approach

This report was motivated by a desire to better understand U.S.-China relations over the critical issue of cybersecurity. Three basic policy options exist for the United States in dealing with China over this issue: to focus primarily on improving U.S. cyber defenses, to attempt to convince China to change its behavior via diplomacy and/or negotiations over norms and behavior, or to compel China to change its cyber practices through coercion.[30]

Bolstering U.S. defenses is one key policy option, as scholars and policy analysts have noted.[31] This has been going on for a number of years and should certainly be continued. However, such an approach does not seek to address the source of the attacks; indeed, bolstering defenses is recommended, regardless of the source of the cyber threat. To manage the cyber issue within a bilateral relationship, the United States and China must find a way to reach a modus vivendi (i.e., a negotiated agreement) on such issues. On the basis of such considerations, we decided to explore options that went beyond simply improving U.S. cyber defenses.

Similarly, we did not systematically investigate the option of coercing China to the negotiating table. To be sure, the United States could seek to escalate its own imposition of costs for China through a set of responses that might include a mix of public shaming and

---

[29] See, for example, Greg Austin, "No Easy Solutions in U.S.-China Cyber Security," *East Asia Forum*, October 6, 2015. For more on the authors' take on these developments, which occurred as this report was going to press, see the Postscript section of this report.

[30] These options may not be mutually exclusive. For example, the United States could try to shame China into changing its behavior while also offering it some sort of negotiated arrangement; similarly, the United States could seek to improve its defenses (deterrence by denial) while also pressing China to negotiate.

[31] See, for example, Jeffrey Carr, "Cyber Attacks: Why Retaliating Against China Is the Wrong Reaction," *The Diplomat*, August 6, 2015.

threats,[32] indictments against individual Chinese hackers,[33] sanctions against Chinese firms,[34] or even a campaign of debilitating cyberattacks, all of which accept greater risk and thereby hopes to persuade the PRC to see negotiations as a way to lessen the pain and reduce the prospect of a further deterioration of relations.[35] An approach based on coercion was certainly not the Obama administration's first choice, but having seen lower-cost, lower-risk initiatives fail to bring China to the negotiating table, the United States appears to have concluded over the course of 2014–2015 that it needed to increase the pressure on China to see results. As President Obama said of the cyber issue with China during his speech to NSA employees on September 11, 2015: "We can choose to make this an area of competition—which I guarantee you we'll win if we have to—or, alternatively, we can come to an agreement in which we say, this isn't helping anybody; let's instead try to have some basic rules of the road in terms of how we operate."[36]

Still, such an approach carries the risk of escalating conflict even into the physical world or severely damaging U.S. efforts to elicit Chinese cooperation on other fronts, such as addressing climate change, preventing proliferation of weapons of mass destruction technology, stabilizing the global economy, or countering violent extremism. It is unclear whether China would believe that such actions were being taken simply for the purpose of coercing them to negotiations or whether they would instead view the actions simply as an escalation of what some in China are prepared to see as an already ongoing (if unacknowledged) cold war or "Silent Contest," as one recent PLA National

---

[32] "Obama Raises Spectre of Future Cyber War Ahead of Xi Jinping's Visit, Promises That China Cannot Win," *South China Morning Post*, September 12, 2015.

[33] Ellen Nakashima, "Indictment of PLA Hackers Is Part of Broad U.S. Strategy to Curb Chinese Cyberspying," *Washington Post*, May 22, 2014.

[34] Ellen Nakashima, "U.S. Developing Sanctions Against China over Economic Spying," *Washington Post*, August 30, 2015c.

[35] Mastro discusses the need to accept greater risk in confronting Chinese assertiveness. See Oriana Skylar Mastro, "Why Chinese Assertiveness Is Here to Stay," *Washington Quarterly*, Vol. 37, No. 4, winter 2015, pp. 151–170.

[36] David Jackson, "Obama, China's Xi to Hold Tense Meetings on Cybersecurity, Military," *USA Today*, September 21, 2015.

Defense University video terms the relationship between China and the United States.[37] Some forms of cyberattack (e.g., against China's so-called Great Firewall) could just as easily be interpreted as an effort to assault the country's sovereignty or even undermine the CPC's rule and engage in regime change.[38] Finally, on a more practical level, we did not believe that we could find much data to evaluate the merits of such an approach; Chinese writings do not shed much light on the issue, and Chinese interlocutors would presumably not be eager to provide much in the way of useful data that could contribute to assessing such a course of action. While we were aware of this option and considered it at some length, our research did not *systematically* explore such an approach.

Instead, we sought primarily to evaluate the prospects that the United States and China might negotiate their way to yes or find some way to agree on norms and behavior in cyberspace. As noted above, this report seeks to answer two questions spurred by the cancellation of the formal U.S.-China Cyber Working Group: What would be required to restart some sort of official negotiations between the United States and China in cyberspace? And if talks were to resume, what kind of trades are possible between the United States and China over conduct in cyberspace? In the course of addressing these two questions, we also touch on topics (such as the U.S. deterrence posture in cyberspace) that are not necessarily part of any trades but that may influence the process of coming to an understanding between the two countries.

Our methodology has several components. First, we reviewed the relevant secondary-source literature on the subject of Chinese views of cybersecurity and the impact of cybersecurity on U.S.-China relations to inform our understanding of the state of the subject at the point when we began our research. We also organized a roundtable with U.S.-based subject-matter experts to collect insights from those who were either leading China specialists or technically proficient cyber-policy experts or, in some cases, possessed both backgrounds. We also

---

[37] Perlez, 2013.

[38] Zhi Linfei, "Commentary: U.S. Should Think Twice Before Retaliating Against China over Unfounded Hacking Charges," Xinhua, August 3, 2015.

leveraged substantial open-source reporting on the issue by leading media outlets and exchanged views with specialist colleagues.

Second, we sought to understand China's positions by examining the writings of academics and analysts working in think tanks attached to Chinese ministries. While these sources are not always definitive, they enabled us to characterize the general parameters of China's views on cyberspace-related issues. Moreover, as research by the China expert Michael Swaine has shown, since cyberspace is a relatively sensitive topic in China, few Chinese analysts write about it in ways that diverge substantially from government policy. This means that the gap between official and unofficial views, and, hence, that the dangers of mistaking the latter for the former, are relatively small.[39]

Third, we reviewed the history of Track Two negotiations on cyberspace between the United States and China (most notably the dialogue held since 2009 between the American think tank CSIS and CICIR). Collectively, the two primary investigators of this study have participated in all nine rounds of the CSIS-CICIR dialogue, which provided a substantial source of insights and experience to draw on.

Fourth, in May 2015, we traveled to Beijing to conduct interviews with more than 30 individuals, including Chinese academics, think-tank analysts, military officers, and government officials. Our interlocutors were specialists ranging across a broad array of issues directly and more tangentially related to U.S.-China relations in cyberspace, including experts focused on U.S.-China relations, cyber policy, arms-control experts, military strategists, government officials tasked with the cybersecurity account, and observers focused on Chinese economic development strategy. We also benefitted from the opportunity to exchange views with visiting Chinese cybersecurity experts who passed through Washington, D.C., as well as with Lu Wei, the director of the Cyber Administration of China, when he visited the United States in December 2014 and delivered a public address at George Washington

---

[39] Michael D. Swaine, "Chinese Views of Cybersecurity in Foreign Relations," *China Leadership Monitor*, No. 42, fall 2013.

University.[40] In this report, we will refer to some of the interviewees who carried official government titles as *high-level interlocutors* and to everyone else as *respondents*.

Organization of This Report

Chapter Two, "Coming to Terms," lays the groundwork for understanding the two sides' positions on cybersecurity issues by describing two ideal types differentiated by how different countries might understand norms, power, and the role and interests of the state. To state our bottom line up front, adherents of *Red deterrence* regard norms as a reflection of the underlying power balance and the interests of the state, whereas adherents of *Blue deterrence* tend to view norms as more akin to neutral, mutually agreed-upon rules and red lines that serve the common good of all the actors in the international system. As subsequent chapters will argue, such differences in perspectives on the character and role of norms have important implications for each side's understanding of the other side's actions in and attitudes toward cyberspace.

Chapter Three, "Getting to Now," looks at the issues that separate the United States and China in cyberspace: their essential features, the U.S. portrayal of these issues, and China's perspectives on these issues. The chapter draws on our review of relevant Western secondary-source literature, our analyses of Chinese writings on cybersecurity, and the results of past attempts to make progress on cybersecurity through the CSIS-CICIR Track Two dialogues and the official Cyber Working Group.

Chapter Four, "Getting to Yes," is based on our interviews with Chinese respondents and high-level interlocutors. In some cases, we report directly on what we heard. In other cases, we use the material to consider alternative negotiating approaches (e.g., bilateral versus multilateral, synchronous versus asynchronous) and postures.

---

[40] "China's Head of Cyberspace Discusses How to Build Mutual Trust with U.S.," *GW Today*, December 3, 2014.

Chapter Five, "Conclusions," summarizes the research findings and explores options for achieving U.S. cybersecurity policy objectives vis-à-vis China.

CHAPTER TWO

Coming to Terms

In conducting our research, we strove to understand some fundamental differences in the way the United States and China approach norms. To this end, we developed a heuristic set of ideal types. *Red deterrence* is an ideal type that fits many elements of China's view of the role of norms and the role of deterrence in ensuring that others abide by these norms. *Blue deterrence* is an ideal type that fits many elements of the U.S. view of the role of norms and the role of deterrence in ensuring that others abide by these norms. Although we take examples from China's behavior to describe Red deterrence and examples from U.S. behavior to describe Blue deterrence, we do not assert that China's behavior always conforms to Red deterrence—nor does U.S. behavior always conform to Blue deterrence. In a nutshell, to the extent that China adheres to Red deterrence, its leaders, we will argue, believe that the current international system is based on a distribution of power and interests that serves the United States and the West, and the norms that constitute the international order reflect the interests of the United States, the hegemonic power that established the system.

In contrast, to the extent that the United States adheres to Blue deterrence, its officials will view the international order as based on a liberal, inclusive, and fair set of practices that have, over time, been codified in the form of a set of laws and norms that, to a large extent, serve to balance and protect the interests of almost all the actors in the international system. Although the differences between these two ideal types are by no means absolute—Chinese thinkers understand the utility of law (and China's government often quotes the language of the

UN charter), and few Americans doubt that law rests on a foundation of power—the differences in emphasis are nonetheless quite profound.

In this chapter, we first explore the nature and provenance of those differences. In doing so, we define norms as specifying the lines that divide two types of behavior: that which is desirable and that which is forbidden or illegitimate. We then employ the concepts of international voice (or *guoji huayu quan*), deterrence, and compellence to describe how norms are enforced and reinforced. We conclude the discussion by exploring how these differences in U.S. and Chinese views of the enforcement of norms apply to the two countries' views of the nature of their relations in cyberspace.

The Dimensions and Implications of Divergent Views of Deterrence

Blue deterrence thinking tends to take as its starting point the existing international order and seeks to preserve, protect, and further perfect this order. A country that, like the United States, relies on a Blue deterrence model, exercises substantial normative, ideational, and definitional power, expressed both unilaterally and through international organizations, to shape broad consensus on acceptable and unacceptable behavior in international society. To support these normative and rules-based claims, Blue deterrence focuses primarily on describing behavior in terms of normative legitimacy and illegitimacy and only as a secondary step tends to refer to the material strength of the forces that stand in support of these norms. In part, this view of norms is consistent with having the material capacity to impose substantial costs on almost any actor in the international system (as the United States does) but choosing to gain support for its power by imposing some limits on itself to gain buy-in to the system from weaker actors.[1]

Blue deterrence also conforms to an image of a world of peers, where objections to another country's behavior are converted into

---

[1]   G. John Ikenberry, *After Victory: Institutions, Strategic Restraint, and the Rebuilding of Order After Major Wars*, Princeton, N.J.: Princeton University Press, 2000.

accusations that the other country violated commonly accepted laws imposed over what would otherwise be an anarchic world system. It works not through arbitrary authority but through a regime of threat enforced by unilateral or sometimes multilaterally organized punishment administered in a law-like manner. Crossing a no-go line, such as breaking the law, requires punishment if a norm is to be preserved, whether the affected country is an ally or even an unaligned third country (e.g., Kuwait in August 1990).

Such an approach thus conflates the question of what acts constitute acts of war and must be punished with the question of whether punishment against such acts is in a country's interest.[2] Implicit in that inquiry is that whatever no-go line is established must accord with a broader notion of what no-go line may be appropriate for everyone to respond to. The law for one is the law for all. But one reason that Blue can adopt the belief in or rhetoric that supports a law-related approach to deterrence is that it has considerable influence over what such law says (and *in extremis,* it can always exempt itself). Thus, adherence is contingent rather than absolute; weaker countries lack this luxury.[3]

Red deterrence is focused more on the relationship of ideas to the interests of those in power, and the relationship of one actor's power vis-à-vis other powerful actors in the system. It also, archetypically, carries an assumption that, in most cases, the interests between the various actors in the system will be in conflict. Indeed, China's own approach to deterrence tends to assume that, in most cases, the most powerful actor or actors in the system will attempt to cover up the differences between its interests and those of other weaker actors by employing normative language that suggests there is only one legitimate mode of behavior that serves the interests of all actors in the system, pushing a false consciousness that seeks to confuse or compel weaker actors to

---

[2] International law does not talk of "acts of war," but of the "use of force" and "armed attack." We have observed, however, that colloquial analysis of cyberwar asks, "Is this an act of war?" to suggest that certain actions in cyberspace deserve or even impel a warlike response.

[3] For instance, the United States may adhere to a law when its interests are otherwise served because doing so is the price for getting others to adhere to other laws that do not always work in their interests.

accept the legitimacy of their lower status by inducing them to buy into, or concede to, norms that do not really serve their interests. Red deterrence lives in a world defined less by peer actors and more by hierarchy, in which states approach each other as having either greater or lesser degrees of interest in supporting particular norms. Since these are seen much more as reflections of underlying power relationships and interests than as neutral rules that maintain system stability, Red deterrence regards norms with a high degree of skepticism, and its adherents seek to calculate benefits and losses rather than rights and wrongs. It does not assume that norms that sustain the broad international system are necessarily inherently good as currently constructed. Chinese thinkers, accordingly, are very much attuned to the overall correlation of forces (e.g., including diplomatic influence and economic power) among the leading powers of the international system. Thus, they exhibit lower degrees of concern or willingness to respond to violations of norms, since these are assumed to be primarily reflections of the interests of hegemonic powers and not reflective of the interests of the international community as a whole. One consequence of such views is that such notions as the credibility of the international system are less important, since the system as a whole is not seen as carrying nearly as much importance. Instead, the interests of the specific actor are considered more directly in relation to how a given action would affect the balance of power between two countries.

In practice, although China recognizes some virtues in the rule of law, it often complains that many of the laws and norms that govern the international system were drafted in an era in which China was strategically prostrate or weak. Since the law has always been and will always be influenced by the distribution of power—new laws and norms should, in short order, begin to reflect China's new, greater power within the international order. China has observed that the United States is the only country that cannot be (effectively) sanctioned.

Blue and Red models of deterrence are based on competing interests and perceptions about how countries should behave. The differences need not imply a clash; a lot depends on each side's willingness to abjure actions it feels entitled to take because of objections from the other. But the odds of a misunderstanding are likely to rise to the extent that the United States thinks China's behavior is cynical (for favoring power over rules) and that China thinks that U.S. behavior is hypocritical (for using rules to mask power).

Sources of Difference

Blue deterrence reflects the U.S. experience during the Cold War, during which each side could destroy the other—regardless of which side had the greater destructive power at its fingertips. No one doubted that a nuclear strike would call forth a nuclear counterstrike, but the tricky questions involved other circumstances under which nuclear weapons might be used. Left to be determined was how countries established and indicated their no-go lines and what they did to convince their enemies (and assure their friends) that they would, in fact, use nuclear weapons in situations where they threatened (or promised) to do so. Despite analytic efforts to think through limiting nuclear war once it had started, there was little confidence that limitations would be effective soon enough (before millions were killed), if at all. Such concerns gave rise to the emphasis on ensuring that *no* nuclear weapon was ever used.

In contrast, Red deterrence is consistent with the assessments made by China's leaders of their country's experiences during what they characterize as the "century of humiliation," which took place between 1840 and 1949, when foreign powers imposed on the Qing dynasty that ruled before its 1911 fall, after which China collapsed into civil disorder and war between 1912 and 1949. During the "century of humiliation," the Qing dynasty and its successor state, the Republic of China, had no effective way of warding off depredations from economically advanced outsiders, whether from Europe, Russia, or Japan. When the CPC came to power, its goal was to build up the power of the state and thereby gain control over China's destiny—and, as it grew stronger, generate sufficient respect from abroad to win deference for its own interests (even if at a substantial cost to the interests of its neighbors).

Competing conceptions of society form a deep foundation for the differences. In the United States, the autonomous individual is considered the basic unit of social organization and is imbued with the right to make decisions subject to the constraints arising from his or her interaction with others. These constraints are codified in law.

In contrast, in China, a totalitarian communist order was overlaid atop more traditionalist Confucian-Legalist social thought, with all three prioritizing the power of the state and society over the individual. Moreover, these traditions assert that the rightful power of the government should know no formal restraints vis-à-vis the citizens, a notion captured most clearly in the concept of the "people's democratic dictatorship" and the Chinese government's recently expressed view that constitutionalism, or the idea that a government should be constrained by the law, is a threat to the regime.[4] Within the traditional Confucian social framework, individuals are granted a certain level of authority over others according to their place in society. Such relationships are expected to be internalized, and this internalization, in turn, minimizes the necessity explicit use of power to gain compliance.

As previous research on Chinese military thought has shown, the word *deterrence* [*weishe*] is not native to Chinese and translates as something close to a combination of Western *deterrence* with an added layer of *coercion* or *compellence*.[5] These differences may arise less from the limitations of translation and more from the different historical circumstances that Chinese and Western societies have experienced. Blue deterrence reflects the U.S. experiences in the Cold War and Europe's experiences with the notion of the balance of power. Red deterrence reflects China's different experience during the Cold War, where it saw deterrence as a term imposed in defense of an order that it regarded as

---

[4] Vaughan Winterbottom, "In China, Constitutionalism Is a Dirty Word," *The Interpreter*, January 28, 2014; Chris Buckley, "China Takes Aim at Western Ideas," *New York Times*, August 19, 2013.

[5] Joe McReynolds, "Chinese Thinking on Cyber Deterrence," in Philip C. Saunders and Andrew Scobell, eds., *PLA Influence on Chinese National Security Policymaking*, Stanford, Calif.: Stanford University Press, 2015.

illegitimate, undesirable, and imposed on China at great expense to the country's interests.[6]

Blue deterrence aims at stability, which is consistent with the needs of a status quo country. Red deterrence aims at countering hegemony when weak in the name of general principles and then becoming a hegemon when sufficiently strong, so that interests are always taken into account when other countries make choices. Or, as China's then–Foreign Minister Yang Jiechi said in 2010, "China is a big country . . . and other countries are small countries and that is just a fact."[7]

Elements of Difference

For Blue, deterrence is something that either does or does not exist. In theory, it could exist for everyone simultaneously if no country crosses another country's no-go lines out of a fear of the consequences of doing so. If deterrence falters, those who would maintain deterrence may have to restate or redefine their no-go lines and back up their words with costly signals and/or deeds. A signal can involve manipulating force elements (e.g., moving ships and planes), but it need not mean using force itself. Blue deterrence pays a great deal of attention to no-go lines. These lines should be so clear that third parties could reliably judge behavior relative to such no-go lines—both in terms of what others cannot do but also in terms of what others can think they can get away with. Blue deterrence assumes that clearly conveying to others what one will defend minimizes the possibility of war as a consequence of error or misjudgment.

Red deterrence abjures no-go lines in favor of a measure of strategic ambiguity designed to magnify the influence of a weaker hand by expanding the zone of uncertainty about what sorts of actions might trigger a response. By design, the ambiguity of what lines, if crossed,

---

[6]   Dean Cheng, "Chinese Views on Deterrence," *Joint Forces Quarterly*, No. 60, spring 2011, pp. 92–94.

[7]   "The Dragon's New Teeth," *The Economist*, April 7, 2012.

will lead to conflict makes things more complicated for other powers while simultaneously giving the weaker power (e.g., China) strategic flexibility to decline to act should it conclude that an action would damage its interests, but it lacks the power to punish the actor who committed the act. Such an approach encourages other countries to take into account a powerful country's views on what exactly constitutes a no-go line, to pause before acting, and to calculate the risks of conflict over their actions across a broader spectrum than might be the case if such a country specified its interests more clearly.

In practice, China typically has not drawn clear no-go lines so much as it has indicated an increasing irritation with the acts of others that go too far in its view. In an important sense, Chinese deterrence has been comparatively retrospective, implicit, and analog (the degree of irritation is a function of how far the other side has gone). By contrast, U.S. deterrence has aimed to be comparatively prospective (spelled out in advance), explicit, and digital (one either crosses the no-go line or not). Moreover, as the strategy of a weaker but dissatisfied power, Red deterrence tends to involve not only elements of compulsion, but also efforts to create the perception among foreign audiences that a country has a high level of risk acceptance out of a belief that deterrence involves both capabilities and the willingness to run the chance of war.[8] In contrast, Blue deterrence tends to be aimed at avoiding the possibility of accidental or unintended conflict and seeks to return the situation to precrisis stability.

Red deterrence has a strong element of reminding others where they stand in the pecking order of international power distribution. China has constantly reminded others of the need to respect Chinese interests and power. Both China's war against India in 1962 and its invasion of Vietnam in 1979 were used to remind its neighbors of what it can (and would) do if its interests were challenged. Its 1996 missile volleys off the northern and southern port cities of Taiwan grew from

---

[8]   Cheng, 2011. Mastro, 2015, highlights China's efforts to use risk manipulation and to create an impression of high levels of risk acceptance to expand its ability to shape foreign governments' policy decisions.

the same imperatives (until the United States intervened to communicate its own power).

When war looms, China's narrative has pointed to the necessity of using force to compel others to accord China its due respect. The purpose of war is to demonstrate the basis for such respect (i.e., "we told you to respect our interests; now we will force you to"). For this reason, China has found that it had to carefully calculate the balance of forces before it set out to demonstrate them. In contrast, U.S. analysts see war arising from the inability to communicate either the no-go lines and/or the credibility of its threats. A purpose of force is to reinforce such intentions (i.e., "we told you not to do this, you did this, and now we have to use punishment to make the point").

For the United States, it has been important to keep some punishment capability in reserve, particularly if the country wanted to maintain some element of deterrence after initial punishment. Thus, punishment has to be calibrated in every case when the other side is expected to survive immediate application of punishment. For China, calibration was less important because the point of applying power was not for China to modulate the behavior of other countries but for it to emphasize China's power; weaker countries were then expected to modulate their own behavior in deference. Stronger countries, on the other hand, understand that China would not submit meekly, despite the differential in their relative amounts of power.

If Blue deterrence treats compellence as different from deterrence, even as Red sees them as two sides of the same coin, this is because Blue deterrence more closely approximates a law-enforcement model that fits with a system-organizing and sustaining power, while Red deterrence is more premised on assumptions about the nature of power, fear, and order. Blue deterrence limits punishment to sins of commission. If the deterrence works, no one transgresses. The narrative of compellence—which requires a country to do something or face punishment—does not fit the transgression model so easily; it is a sin of omission, which is quite different. The distinction also recognizes the autonomy of the other side. Those who do not cross no-go lines can argue that they were not coerced—they simply had no intention of crossing the no-go line in question in the first place. In contrast, those who would be punished for failing to do something and therefore find themselves forced to do it under duress will be much more likely to be seen as having been coerced. Red deterrence is based on deference to another country's will, almost irrespective of issue. Whether the use of power is to keep another country from moving forward or making them move back is secondary. What matters is the degree to which a country's will can be imposed on others. In imposing its will, little concession is granted to the notion of actors' rights to decisionmaking autonomy; indeed, Red deterrence would prefer that submission be seen by the other country (if not necessarily by third parties) as exactly that.

Blue deterrence thought sees international stability arising from the universal adherence to a set of norms related to what one country can do to another; it is enforced by actions taken against norm violators. Red deterrence finds stability in the universal acknowledgment of a global power hierarchy (i.e., the international distribution of power or the pecking order) that dictates patterns of deference. Both forms of deterrence rely on proscription and the power to enforce it, but Blue deterrence emphasizes the proscription, while Red deterrence emphasizes the power.

Law and Equality

Red deterrence appeals to narratives that emphasize the righteousness of weaker countries maneuvering in a world of powerful countries (with imperialist pasts). But a narrative strategy based on antihegemony has a tricky turn to make if a country gains enough power to be a hegemon itself. Such signifiers as *sovereignty* and *hegemony*, are, after all, highly situation dependent in application; thus, when the situation changes, a country's interests will also change, although not its understanding of how the game is and should be played. It is precisely because such turns are tricky that Red must engage in psychological operations more consciously (and perhaps conscientiously) than Blue does. The latter's job is easier, since the laws and norms it champions can survive its advocate's descent from or ascent to hegemonic status.

The Red deterrence attitude toward law therefore presents potential contradictions. On the one hand, insisting on a rule of law in common domains, such as cyberspace, is a good way to curb the behavior of others; when the law is applied to oneself, a common response is to fall behind claims of sovereignty (that is, a country can operate by its own laws) and call for mutual trust. On the other hand, if a country does become a hegemon, it may find that there are some international laws and norms that it cannot reshape to its own advantage. Thus, prior lip service to the concept of international laws and norms may become the sort of constraint that would not exist in a world in which acceptable behavior was defined primarily by who had what power.

Separately, China and the United States have tended to use the concept of "equality" differently. The United States believes it treats other nations as equals because they have equal standing before international law and norms. In contrast, China complains that it is not treated as an equal by the United States because it garners insufficient respect from the United States as a country of comparable power (which it is not).[9]

Blue deterrence easily lends itself to alliances because it is easy to extend the unilateral enforcement of universal norms to a multilateral enforcement regime. The United States can even maintain that alliances join together as equals and that alliances operate under voting principles (even if everyone understands who really has the power within an alliance). Red deterrence does not lend itself as easily to alliances because its world is not really one of nominal peers much less of actual peers; everyone is either up or down relative to one another. China may have states with which it shares common interests or even formal allies. In those relationships, if China is powerful, the aligned states are essentially seen as supplicants locked into asymmetric relationships. Thus, the aligned states are unlikely to be allies of one another, since they are not linked by a desire to defend common values so much as a shared or common dependency on China.

---

[9] Various interviewees, Beijing, May 2015.

The Application of Different Deterrence Approaches to Cyberspace

Differences between Blue and Red deterrence models are reflected in current controversies over cyberspace. To illustrate as much, consider the concepts of hegemony, attribution, escalation, stability, and norms as they may apply in cyberspace and as they are reflected in American and Chinese approaches.

Hegemony

China remains very concerned, perhaps obsessed, with cyberspace hegemony—the ability of certain countries to get their way consistently in cyberspace, while others have to play by rules set by hegemons. U.S. officials and experts do not talk (and may not even think) in terms of hegemony but assume that countries, if playing under fair and reasonable rules (whose provenance is held to be irrelevant) will be able to achieve their legitimate aims in cyberspace much as in the physical world.

Could China someday become a cyberspace hegemon? What is it about the United States that has made it, in Chinese observers' views, a cyberspace hegemon? If the U.S. advantage lies with its inherent national capabilities (e.g., education, capital), China's path to usurping U.S. hegemony should be straightforward and legitimate: more spending on education and more support to innovation. But Chinese thinkers also appear to believe that the United States holds unfair advantages in cyberspace as a function of having invented the relevant technologies that made the Internet—an advantage fairly won but unfairly extended. U.S.-based Internet governance groups, such as ICANN (a nonprofit corporation that serves to manage certain aspects of domain-name registration on the Internet) and, to a lesser extent, the Internet Engineering Task Force (an open-membership organization that promotes common, voluntary Internet standards) are also targets of China's ire.

The United States resists reforming these organizations in a direction that would take consideration of China's interests because it reasons that China's preferred rules for cyberspace would come at the expense of Internet freedom. For its part, China believes that Internet freedom is an essential element of U.S. hegemony and a direct threat to the ruling status of the CPC. To better insulate itself from the perceived threat of U.S.-inspired Internet-based subversion, China has expressed an interest in building a direct Asia-to-Europe fiber-optic cable connection to avoid sending its Internet traffic across servers based in the United States (where Chinese observers worry it will be intercepted or potentially, in case of a conflict, blocked).

Similarly, China wants to leverage its internal market to promote the proliferation of technical standards with a distinct made-in-China look to favor Chinese companies. China therefore makes determined efforts to displace what it calls the eight *guardian warriors* of U.S. Internet hegemony (Cisco, IBM, Google, Qualcomm, Intel, Apple, Oracle, and Microsoft).[10] Yet, as successful as Chinese firms have been in making serious inroads into hardware markets (e.g., Huawei routers, ZTE handsets, Xiaomi cell phones), the country's firms have enjoyed far less success in the software market. The latter requires an ability to invent or reinvent new things for computers and devices to do. It also benefits from network effects (i.e., yesterday's leader establishes the conventions that attract people to align with the current leader, thereby making yesterday's leader a future leader). Neither the capacity to innovate (in contrast with making marginal improvements to an existing design) nor the ability to leverage prior market success is considered a Chinese comparative advantage.

Another problem for China in cyberspace is that, while it might aspire to be the East Asian hegemon in the physical world, it makes no sense to be the East Asian hegemon in cyberspace. What level of hegemony need it achieve in cyberspace? Does it suffice to nullify whatever advantages the United States reaps from being a global hegemon in cyberspace, or should it try to establish some sort of regional autarky in cyberspace?

---

[10] Carlos Tejada, "Microsoft, the 'Guardian Warriors' and China's Cybersecurity Fears," *Wall Street Journal*, July 29, 2014.

Attribution Versus the Correlation of Forces

Confidence in the ability to determine who carried out a cyberattack is very important for the law-enforcement approach that characterizes Blue deterrence; some observers even talk of needing to meet evidentiary standards of guilt that go beyond a reasonable doubt before meting out punishment. Confidence in attribution is less important for Red deterrence, which is more concerned about the ability to retaliate and prevail against those it would retaliate against.

For Red, the question is not "Can we prove that country X did this?" but rather "Can we afford to impose punishment on the presumed attacker? And if we do so, who will come out on top? Conversely, even if victory is unlikely, can we afford not to push back if the insults from being successfully attacked create the impression of powerlessness?" Under such circumstances, the appropriate metric for evaluating Red's calculus of retaliation is not its degree of confidence in correctly targeting the actual attacker but more one of assessing relative power differentials and ability to benefit from the retaliation and thereby recover its reputation. Red is thus more likely to respond in reaction to a pattern of attacks that shifts or indicates a possible impending shift in the balance of power and that therefore must be opposed. In contrast, Blue is more likely to retaliate based solely on one attack, especially one that, if left unpunished, threatens the rule of law in cyberspace.

The United States remains frustrated that China resolutely refuses to acknowledge the cyberattacks it carries out, despite a plethora of evidence that it has done so. In U.S. eyes, China is lawless. In China's eyes, U.S. efforts to force an admission are ploys to force China to concede to U.S. hegemony in cyberspace.

Escalation

Restraining the other side's impulse to escalate in cyberspace during a conflict raises issues similar to those of deterring an initial attack. The major difference is that, during a conflict, the standards for attribution are likely to be lower than with respect to deterrence during peacetime. For Blue, the ability and willingness to react quickly when such thresholds are breached are essential, lest today's unanswered violation come to be seen as the new normal level of "acceptable" cyberattacks (within the context of a broader overall conflict).

Red assumes conflict in cyberspace is one aspect of an overall struggle that is an ever-present aspect of international society, even if, at times, it is useful to downplay or deny entirely the existence of such struggles. Such a country may well want to limit the scope of the conflict and/or try to convince others that no such conflict exists to encourage them to lower their guard, protect its reputation, or decrease the likelihood that it might suffer retaliation (or a combination of these three motives). Overall, Red seeks to adjust the level of conflict to that which best plays to its advantage. Red would thus be less likely to use carrots and sticks (inducements and punishments) in an attempt to regulate the exact nature of cyberattacks by Blue. As long as one side is more relaxed about individual violations of perceived norms, a confrontation between two countries is less likely to result in uncontrolled escalation, because each side attempts to match (much less overmatch) the others' violations to persuade the other side to stay within limits. This behavior is consistent with the realities of cyberattacks, notably their subordination to other forms of conflict and the difficulty of determining with any precision which attacks crossed which thresholds.

Nevertheless, the same event may elicit different reactions by both sides. Blue may react sharply to an act by Red that seems to expand the scope of acceptable cyberwar (e.g., by putting new targets in play or by introducing corruption into systems that were previously only disrupted). This reaction may surprise Red's self-assessment that the move did not reflect a difference in power relationships (e.g., it did not change the narrative of the conflict or the relationship between the two countries). Red may react sharply to an attack by Blue that alters power relationships (e.g., by reducing Red's internal stability or souring relationships between it and other countries) and thus surprise Blue, which thought it was not striking any targets hitherto off limits (or using cyberattack methods that were considered off limits). Significant differences in what each side considers escalatory can lead to an escalation on each side because it thought the other side did when neither side, itself, had intended to do so.

Stability

Both sides have an interest in cyberspace stability (the absence of conditions that encourage cyberattacks or kinetic wars that start with real or presumed cyberattacks). Yet, each side may seek stability in its own way. The United States has maintained that the creation and adherence to limits coupled, as they must be, with the understood determination of the United States to enforce these limits are what create stability. But unless countries give potential attackers the benefit of the doubt, what looks like a cyberattack—but what may be an accident or a mistaken assessment that an instance of cyber espionage is in fact an indicator of an imminent cyberattack—may trigger conflict in a world where each side is primed to retaliate against the trespasses of others.[11] China would maintain that a well-understood hierarchy of power creates a consensus on the outcome of challenging the existing order, since no actor in the system has any reason to believe it can ultimately benefit from mounting such a challenge. In theory, such an approach could result in increased turbulence during a time when hegemony is passing from one country (which still insists on its perquisites) to another (which challenges the perquisites). However, inasmuch as activity in cyberspace is a subset of the broad set of power indicators, perturbations that might challenge *only* the existing order in cyberspace may matter little when calculating the broader correlation of forces.

Signaling

Problems could also arise if the United States attempts to read China's signals and forgets (or chooses not to recognize) that China sees deterrence within its own framework—and vice versa. The United States may read China's acts as trying to break rules or establish different rules of international behavior; China may see U.S. actions as forcing China to concede to the desired power position of the United States. The May 2014 indictment of five officers from the Chinese PLA may

---

[11] For instance, what initially looked like a North Korean insertion of malware into the networks of South Korea's nuclear power plants turned out to be some random malware circulating through the Internet that hopped onto internal networks (nuclear plant controls were not touched); see Meeyoung Cho, "Low-Risk 'Worm' Removed at Hacked South Korea Nuclear Operator," Reuters, December 30, 2014.

have been seen by the United States as a signal that individuals who behave contrary to U.S. law cannot do so with impunity. The Chinese, however, may have read the indictments as an attempt by the United States to demonstrate its extraterritorial power and thereby violate Chinese sovereignty—and China's ending its Track One talks on cybersecurity was its way of pushing back.[12]

Likewise, the United States has appealed to China to crack down on North Korea's use of the Internet as a way of signaling to North Korea that destructive (or at least highly disruptive) attacks on international corporations goes beyond acceptable practice. But China, as far as has been reported, has been reluctant to press North Korea. China's leadership may view North Korea's association with the Sony hack as a very small part of a much broader relationship—whereas any action China takes may be viewed as a big deal and indicative that China has bowed to U.S. pressure.

The broader point is that Blue deterrence responds to transgressions, while Red deterrence is focused on the broader power relationship among countries. A large, perhaps dominant, element of the U.S. desire to punish North Korea is to create a precedent for punishing cyberattacks, irrespective of who carried them out. "Sony is important to me because the entire world is watching how we as a nation are going to respond do this," said ADM Michael S. Rogers, Commander, U.S. Cyber Command (USCYBERCOM), stating further that "if we don't name names here, it will only encourage others to decide, 'Well this must not be a no-go line for the United States.'"[13] China's resistance has little to do with condoning cyberattacks and more to do with worries about its relationships with North Korea and the United States. When it comes to other countries, the United States tends to particularize,

---

[12] Of course, it is also possible that the United States had seen no effect from private representations to the Chinese side over cyber intrusions and so sought to impose a cost on China's actions. In the indictment, Chinese may simply have seen their interests and prestige being challenged and sought to respond in a way designed to stand up for their position and reframe themselves as innocent victims.

[13] Sam Frizell, "NSA Director on Sony Hack: 'The Entire World Is Watching,'" *Time*, January 8, 2015.

while China tends to generalize; when it comes to norms of behavior, the United States tends to generalize, while China particularizes.

Overall

Deterrence between the United States and the Soviet Union for a substantial part of the Cold War was, at least at the nuclear level, based on a rough symmetry of capabilities and mutual understanding of what deterrence meant. Both sides had a rough idea of where each other's no-go lines might be and a rough idea of what each other's response to crossing these no-go lines would be.

In a world of dramatically divergent deterrence models, this may not follow. For Blue, line crossing is an act in and of itself, and the failure to note and react to such a crossing is one in which the rule of law is imperiled. For Red, the line is more like a wide zone, and the response to incursions into that zone is entirely dependent on the context in which the crossing takes place and what such a crossing implies about the other side's understanding of relative power relationships. Transgressions are worth responding to only if they connote that one country's perception of another needs correcting, and that cannot be determined without taking into consideration other events—which may have nothing to do with cyberspace. Indeed, the U.S. calculus on whether to react may depend on events having nothing to do with the last person to cross the line. In the case of Sony, the United States may have also factored in an earlier hack on the Las Vegas Sands Corporation (widely ascribed to Iran) and concluded that something had to be done about the rule of law in cyberspace. China is more likely to link events that take place in cyberspace with the larger context of another country's actions, while the United States is more likely to consider events in cyberspace within the context of this medium. When explaining why North Korea had to be punished for attacking Sony—a policy adopted by the U.S. President—one sees the commander of USCYBERCOM arguing in favor of retaliation because others were watching how we would react to the attack—but one did not see the commander of U.S.

Pacific Command making the case that this was an essential component of the U.S. relationship with North Korea.

A world in which two widely divergent models of deterrence are held by the leading powers of the international system requires that each understand deterrence through the others' eyes. The mental gymnastics required to do so are not only difficult but assume that neither side deems the other side through an exclusively adversarial lens.

CHAPTER THREE

Getting to Now

The relationship between the United States and China has increasingly been affected by what each country thinks the other is doing to it in cyberspace. In this chapter, we review the history of the two countries' relationship in cyberspace and describe the respective perspectives on each other's activities. To do so, we draw on both open-source media reporting and the writings of U.S. and Chinese experts on cybersecurity. We also draw on our participation in nine rounds of CSIS-CICIR Track Two dialogues on cybersecurity.

We begin by detailing U.S. perceptions of China with respect to cybersecurity. U.S. dissatisfaction with Chinese behavior in cyberspace plays a large role in its overall view of China, while China's concerns about U.S. behavior in cyberspace play a substantially more modest role in shaping its overall view of the United States. As one of our Chinese interviewees told us, "the U.S. may regard cybersecurity as one of its top five priorities with China, but for us, it may only be in the top ten or even the top 20 issues we have with you."[1]

The first conflicts between the United States and China over cyberspace were strictly freelance affairs. Following real-world events, such as the bombing of China's embassy in Belgrade in 1999 and the EP-3 incident off Hainan Island in 2001, hackers on both sides labored to deface websites in each other's countries. The results were little more than minor annoyances but served to create and reinforce the impression within the United States that China primarily used proxies to

---

[1] Interview in Beijing, May 2015.

carry out cyberattacks both small and large. Over time, expert U.S. assessments have concluded that China's cyber operations, whether or not they initially employed patriotic "hacktivists," have evolved to be a much more substantially centralized operation, with military and intelligence organizations in command-and-control roles.[2]

China's Cyber Espionage

As both the United States and China invested in networked systems (what the Chinese refer to as *xinxihua* or *informatization*), both sides have committed cyber espionage on each other (and third parties) for multiple purposes. In part because the United States has maintained effective command and control over its hackers, who, in turn, maintained very high standards of operational security, almost everything known about hacking carried out by the United States and China comes from knowledge about Chinese hacking.

The U.S.'s problem with China's activities in cyberspace mounted over a number of years, starting in the early 2000s. Attacks attributed to China include the 2003–2005 Titan Rain penetrations of Department of Energy laboratories, as well as later attacks targeting defense-related institutions, such as the Naval War College and the National Defense University.[3] Such attacks led to extended shutdowns as oversight officers made sure that all systems were thoroughly cleaned out and that no classified data was at risk from exposure. Attacks on the U.S. Department of Commerce (which deals with exports and export controls) resulted in administrators replacing all their machines to recover control over their systems. Another intrusion hit the Department of State.[4] A particularly brazen attack, revealed in 2007, targeted

---

[2]   Brian Krekel, George Bakos, and Christopher Barnett, *Capability of the People's Republic of China to Conduct Cyber Warfare and Computer Network Exploitation*, Washington, D.C.: The U.S.-China Economic and Security Review Commission, 2009; see also Mandiant, 2013; and Nigel Inkster, "Chinese Intelligence in the Cyber Age," *Survival*, Vol. 55, No. 1, February–March 2013, pp. 45–66.

[3]   Nathan Thornburgh, "Inside the Chinese Hack Attack," *Time*, August 25, 2005.

[4]   Christine Lagorio, "State Department Computers Hacked," CBS News, July 11, 2006.

machines at the Pentagon, including the computer personally used by the Secretary of Defense.[5] Additionally, when Senators John McCain and Barack Obama were running as presidential candidates, they were informed that the computer systems in their campaign headquarters had been penetrated by Chinese hackers.[6]

China's reputation as an aggressive actor in cyberspace was cemented with the penetration of Lockheed Martin's F-35 Lightning II program that aimed to exfiltrate several terabytes worth of data.[7] Supposedly, the hackers only took unclassified data, and not a lot of it was useful, as information about the F-35 itself would have been limited. Indeed, China has likely learned far more about making advanced jet aircraft by reverse engineering hardware acquired from Russia. China may have also learned about systems integration in general, but, again, that is speculation. Rumors persist that the aggregation of this purloined unclassified data might have been provided to China with information that was equivalent to top-secret data. In late 2009, Google discovered that it, too had been attacked (notably by having its code repository rifled) by individuals who exfiltrated their take through a server in Taiwan en route to China; this intrusion event was labeled Operation Aurora by the researchers who discovered it. The novel element of the Google attack was the company's willingness to talk about it—and to persuade the U.S. government to raise the incident as an international issue with China. Google was already under pressure from the Chinese government for resisting demands to censor search results while wanting to compete in the Chinese market against Baidu, a search-engine competitor, and Google simultaneously announced that it was suspending its internal China service and transferring Chinese users to their Hong Kong site. This would mean that search results in China would not be censored by Google, even though users would have to pass through the Great Firewall of China when

---

[5]   See for instance, CSIS, "Significant Cyber Incidents Since 2006," March 10, 2014.

[6]   Brendan Sasso, "Report: China Hacked Obama, McCain Campaigns in 2008," *The Hill*, June 7, 2013.

[7]   Siobhan Gorman, August Cole, and Yochi Dreazen, "Computer Spies Breach Fighter-Jet Project," *Wall Street Journal*, April 21, 2009.

making queries. Another series of attacks, nicknamed Shady RAT by the researchers at McAfee who discovered it, showed the industriousness of Chinese hackers. Researchers found a server that housed stolen files from 74 hacked firms, all cached for later delivery.[8] Most, but not all, of these firms were in the United States, and their businesses ranged from industry to commercial real estate.

In 2011, RSA, the company that sells multifactor authentication systems, was hacked. Hackers reportedly managed to break into the systems that maintained RSA's authentication servers, thereby enabling them to break into systems that were protected with RSA products. A few months after the attack, hackers supposedly used information collected from the attack to target Lockheed Martin, although that attack was apparently thwarted.[9]

In 2011, a cyberattack was carried out against oil companies to determine how they evaluated certain oil patches and what they were prepared to bid on them.[10] Such information could be of immense value to competing oil companies, which could then determine what such drilling rights were worth and how to narrowly outbid oil majors when these properties were offered for lease. Law firms, incidentally, have proven to be soft targets for such penetrations because they keep highly privileged data but have traditionally not been the most computer savvy of organizations (or large enough to afford sophisticated information technology staff).[11]

---

[8] The hackers took the files; sent them to another server for accumulation and, at some point, collected them (i.e., "mailed them home"). The files on the server may have been cached for later delivery. In all likelihood, they were not discovered by their original owners but by a third party that specialized in looking for such files; the search was not done in the pay of every organization whose files ended up on the server. The search may have been paid for, however, by one of those organizations.

[9] Matthew J. Schwartz, "Lockheed Martin Suffers Massive Cyberattack," *InformationWeek Dark Reading*, May 30, 2011.

[10] McAfee Foundstone Professional Services and McAfee Labs, *Global Energy Cyberattacks: "Night Dragon,"* white paper, Santa Clara, Calif.: McAfee, February 10, 2011. See also Dmitri Alperovich, *Revealed: Operation Shady RAT,* white paper, Santa Clara, Calif.: McAfee, August 3, 2011.

[11] Michael A. Riley and Sophia Pearson, "China-Based Hackers Target Law Firms to Get Secret Deal Data," Bloomberg, January 31, 2012.

Chinese intrusions are so extensive that Shaun Henry, the former head of the FBI's cybersecurity division, has remarked that, "There are two types of companies: companies that have been breached and companies that don't know they've been breached."[12]

Ironically, poor tradecraft seems to be an issue with the Chinese.[13] The attempts made to hide the trail of malware infiltration or the exfiltration of data do not seem to be very robust. The fact that the files found on intermediate servers are not encrypted means that those who find such files can read them, guess where they came from, and inform the victims, thereby allowing them to staunch the bleeding. Anyone who uses the same method to penetrate 33 companies, à la Aurora, is risking the collapse of their entire intrusion effort when the initial penetration is discovered. In 2012, the NSA circulated estimates that a dozen groups in China are responsible for most of the advanced persistent threat intrusions.[14] Nothing particularly effective was done about the hackers—which may be why they put so little effort into hiding their tracks.

While Chinese press claims that U.S. accusations of cyber espionage are little more than inventions fueled by an outdated U.S. "Cold War mentality,"[15] the United States is not alone in its perception of being under sustained cyber intrusions by Chinese hackers. Accusations have come from Germany (whose prime minister, Angela Merkel, brought this issue up personally with her Chinese counterparts),[16] the

---

[12] Nicole Perlroth, "Nissan Is Latest Company to Get Hacked," *New York Times*, April 24, 2012.

[13] David Kravets, "FBI Director Says Chinese Hackers Are Like a 'Drunk Burglar,'" *Ars Technica*, October 6, 2014. Reportedly, President Xi called for better tradecraft after the June 2013 complaints by President Obama at the Sunnylands summit.

[14] "Twelve Chinese Hacker Groups Responsible for Attacks on U.S.," Homeland Security News Wire, December 16, 2011. A later estimate talked in terms of 20 groups, see Danny Yadron, James T. Areddy, and Paul Mozur, "Chinese Hacking Is Deep and Diverse, Experts Say," *Wall Street Journal*, May 29, 2014.

[15] "China Voice: Drop Cold War Mentality on China's Cybersecurity," Xinhua, April 22, 2014.

[16] "Espionage Report: Merkel's China Visit Marred by Hacking Allegations," *Spiegel* online, August 27, 2012. See also "German Government and Companies Attacked by Chinese

United Kingdom[17] (which warned companies in public against such threats), France,[18] Canada,[19] Australia,[20] Israel,[21] Taiwan,[22] Japan,[23] Association of Southeast Asian Nations,[24] and India.[25]

Finally, cyber espionage is consistent with China's broader approach to intelligence gathering and acquisition of strategically valuable intellectual property. A large number of Chinese individuals have been convicted abroad of physical espionage operations or theft of intellectual property or business proprietary information.[26] For example, only about one in ten copies of Microsoft Windows present in China were assessed to be authentic as of early 2011, with the illegal copies presumably more vulnerable to intrusion, a fact that suggests how penetrable China's infrastructure might be to cyberattacks from

---

Hackers," *Want China Times*, February 26, 2013.

[17] CSIS, 2014.

[18] Eliot Sefton, "Chinese 'Hacked French Ministry for G20 Data,'" *The Week*, March 8, 2011.

[19] "Canada National Research Council 'Hacked by Chinese Spies,'" BBC, July 29, 2014.

[20] Rob Taylor, "Australian Spy HQ Plans Stolen by Chinese Hackers: Report," Reuters, May 27, 2013; Dylan Welch, "Chinese Hackers 'Breach Australian Media Organizations' Ahead of G20," Australian Broadcasting Corporation, November 13, 2014.

[21] Joe Miller, "Israeli Iron Dome Firms 'Infiltrated by Chinese Hackers,'" BBC, July 31, 2014.

[22] Shannon Tiezzi, "Taiwan Complains of 'Severe' Cyber Attacks from China," *The Diplomat*, August 15, 2014.

[23] Monami Yui and Shingo Kawamoto, "Chinese Criminals Blamed for Record Japan Bank Cybertheft," Bloomberg, December 17, 2014.

[24] Tim Culpan, "Decade-Long Cyberspy Attack Hacked Southeast Asian Targets," Bloomberg, April 12, 2015.

[25] John Markoff and David Barboza, "Researchers Trace Data Theft to Intruders in China," *New York Times*, April 5, 2010.

[26] For instance, Yudhijit Bhattacharjee, "A New Kind of Spy: How China Obtains American Technological Secrets," *New Yorker*, May 5, 2014 (about operations against Boeing), and Karen Gullo, "California Man Guilty of Stealing DuPont Trade Secrets," *Bloomberg Business*, March 5, 2014 (about operations against DuPont).

other countries.[27] Applications to import products into or start manufacturing in China are frequently delayed due to demands that corporations release a great deal of their intellectual property to domestic firms before getting permission to enter the Chinese market. A wide range of foreign observers have also accused China of manipulating information technology standards to retain an advantage in its home market and give Chinese companies a head start in penetrating foreign markets.

Another U.S. concern is the fear that Chinese hackers will target U.S. critical infrastructure in an attempt to hold the U.S. society and economy hostage in the event of a major confrontation between the two countries. In 2011, for instance, a Pentagon official attempted to explain to China that its penetration of several natural gas pipeline systems was touching a U.S. red line.[28] The penetration of Telvent, the Canadian company that supplies control systems to the U.S. natural gas sector, also touched a nerve.[29]

In 2013, the Director of National Intelligence deemed a large-scale cyberattack on the nation's critical infrastructure (of which the electric grid is the most prominent part) to be the greatest short-term threat to the nation's security.[30] The next year, the Director of the NSA,

---

[27] In a paper sponsored by Microsoft, Gantz et al. argued that bootleg copies are more prone to malware (nevertheless, consider the source). See John F. Gantz et al., *The Dangerous World of Counterfeit and Pirated Software: How Pirated Software Can Compromise the Cybersecurity of Consumers, Enterprises, and Nations . . . and the Resultant Costs in Time and Money* , Framingham, Mass.: International Data Corporation, 2013,

[28] Mark Clayton, "Exclusive: Cyberattack Leaves Natural Gas Pipelines Vulnerable to Sabotage," *Christian Science Monitor*, February 27, 2013.

[29] Brian Krebs, "Chinese Hackers Blamed for Intrusion at Energy Industry Giant Telvent," *Krebs on Security*, September 12, 2012.

[30] The first page of James R. Clapper, "Statement of Record: Worldwide Threat Assessment of the U.S. Intelligence Community," Washington, D.C.: Director of National Intelligence, February 26, 2015, states

> We judge that there is a remote chance of a major cyberattack against US critical infrastructure systems during the next two years that would result in long-term, wide-scale disruption of services, such as a regional power outage. . . . However . . . less advanced but highly motivated actors could access some poorly protected US networks that con-

ADM Michael S. Rogers, testified that China, and perhaps other countries, could take down the U.S. electric power grid.[31]

The 2011 U.S. International Strategy for Cyberspace

The 2011 U.S. *International Strategy for Cyberspace* describes a world that the United States wants to see but one that clearly require other actors, most notably China, to cease and avoid certain kinds of behavior. It calls on the international community to build consensus around principles of responsible behavior in cyberspace, pointing to the Budapest Convention on Cybercrime (which commits signatories to assist international efforts to solve cybercrimes, including cyber espionage) as an example of what it sees as a useful approach. The *Strategy* held that one norm of responsible behavior was that "States must identify and prosecute cybercriminals . . . ensure laws and practices deny criminals safe havens, and cooperate with international criminal investigations in a timely manner," adding that "States should recognize and act on their responsibility to protect information infrastructures and secure national systems from damage or misuse."[32] Countries should ensure that hackers do not use their networks to attack the systems of other countries or—in light of China's protests that others frequently transit China's poorly secured networks to attack Western targets—ensure that countries secure their networks so well that such transit attacks are impossible.

China's response to the issuance of the *Strategy* focused in part on concerns about how the United States proposes to respond to cyberattacks. The *Strategy* states, on page 10, that "[c]onsistent with the United

---

trol core functions, such as power generation, during the next two years, although their ability to leverage that access to cause high-impact, systemic disruptions will probably be limited. At the same time, there is a risk that unsophisticated attacks would have significant outcomes due to unexpected system configurations and mistakes, or that vulnerability at one node might spill over and contaminate other parts of a networked system.

[31] Dilanian, 2014.

[32] White House, *International Strategy for Cyberspace: Prosperity, Security, and Openness in a Networked World*, Washington, D.C., May 2011, p. 10.

Nations Charter, states have an inherent right to self-defense that may be triggered by certain aggressive acts in cyberspace," and continues with this point on page 14:

> When warranted, the United States will respond to hostile acts in cyberspace as we would to any other threat to our country. All states possess an inherent right to self-defense, and we recognize that certain hostile acts conducted through cyberspace could compel actions under the commitments we have with our military treaty partners. We reserve the right to use all necessary means—diplomatic, informational, military, and economic—as appropriate and consistent with applicable international law, in order to defend our Nation, our allies, our partners, and our interests. In so doing, we will exhaust all options before military force whenever we can; will carefully weigh the costs and risks of action against the costs of inaction; and will act in a way that reflects our values and strengthens our legitimacy, seeking broad international support whenever possible.

The Chinese reacted to this specific paragraph and must have been aware of the declaration of an unnamed U.S. military official: "If you shut down our power grid, maybe we will put a missile down one of your smokestacks."[33]

Mandiant, Snowden, and the PLA 5

A volley of unexpected events rearranged the U.S.-China confrontation in cyberspace in 2013–2014.

February 2013 saw the release of a report by the Mandiant, a cybersecurity company specializing in forensic investigation (subsequently purchased by FireEye), that presented copious evidence that at least one group within the PLA, Unit 61398, was involved with

---

[33] See for instance, Adam Segal, "Chinese Responses to the International Strategy for Cyberspace," Council on Foreign Relations, May 23, 2011; Zhou Wa, "Internet Regulation a Sovereign Issue: FM," *China Daily*, May 20, 2011; and Siobhan Gorman and Julian E. Barnes, "Cyber Combat: Act of War," *Wall Street Journal*, May 31, 2011.

more than 100 different intrusions into 20 different sectors of the U.S. economy dating back as far as early 2006.[34] This was the first public argument that economically motivated cyber espionage (EMCE) could be traced not only to China, but to the Chinese government (rather than to freelance hackers).[35] Since then, other hacker groups have been identified, most of them affiliated with either the PLA or the Chinese Ministry of State Security.[36] Improvements in U.S. attribution capability (in both the public and private sectors) since at least mid-2012 have led to growing tensions between U.S. officials and their Chinese counterparts over the issue of EMCE.[37] The topic was the top item of discussion during the Sunnylands summit of June 2013. Following the summit, NSA advisor Thomas E. Donilon addressed this topic further in a major speech, and Treasury Secretary Jack Lew was dispatched to China to reinforce this point.[38]

On the eve of the summit, however, former NSA contractor Edward Snowden flew from Honolulu to Hong Kong, where he stayed for several days before flying to Russia. After arriving in Hong Kong, Snowden began releasing documents that he alleged revealed key details of the NSA's cyber capabilities and past activities. These documents reinforced the perception of Chinese observers that the United States possessed advanced cyber-espionage capabilities that it had been using on a large scale to penetrate foreign information systems, including a number of targets in China.[39]

---

[34] Mandiant, 2013.

[35] The relevance of this distinction can be inferred from an argument often made by Chinese officials: There are 600 million Chinese on the Internet, and we cannot police them all. Presumably, the Chinese would not argue they could not police employees of the PLA.

[36] See for instance, Novetta, "Cyber Security Coalition Releases Full Report on Large-Scale Interdiction of Chinese State Sponsored Espionage Effort," Washington, D.C., October 28, 2014 (Symantec seems to call the Elderwood Project by its subtitle, *Axiom*).

[37] Nakashima, 2014.

[38] Mark Landler and David E. Sanger, "U.S. Demands China Block Cyberattacks and Agree to Rules," *New York Times*, March 12, 2013.

[39] Te-Ping Chen, "Snowden Alleges U.S. Hacking in China," *Wall Street Journal*, June 23, 2013.

Chinese government officials were able to "dine out" on these revelations.[40] As one commentary in the official Xinhua News Agency put it, "The United States, which has long been trying to play innocent as a victim of cyberattacks, has turned out to be the biggest villain in our age."[41] The Snowden allegations hampered the U.S. effort to mobilize pressure on China and other states to draw a meaningful distinction between traditional espionage against national security targets and EMCE against private sector business interests.

With little progress on the cyber issue resulting from efforts at direct negotiations, U.S. policy toward China's cyber intrusions shifted direction. In May 2014, the U.S. Department of Justice indicted five PLA officers for intrusions into five private sector corporations, in addition to the United Steelworkers.[42] According to press releases about the indictment,[43] six organizations were hacked, and the following were taken:

- from Westinghouse: technical and design specifications for piping and emails associated with the construction of a Chinese facility for a state-owned enterprise
- from Solar World: information about cash flow, manufacturing methods, production-line information, costs, and privileged client-attorney communications related to ongoing trade litigation
- from U.S. Steel: information on servers, probably associated with a trade case against Chinese steel companies

---

[40] "Look Who's Listening," *Economist*, June 15, 2013.

[41] Chen, 2013. See also Lana Lam, "NSA Targeted China's Tsinghua University in Extensive Hacking Attacks, Says Snowden," *South China Morning Post*, June 22, 2013.

[42] Short of war-crimes charges, it is extremely rare for one country to indict military officers of another country for crimes committed in the home country of the accused. Incidentally, the U.S. law under which these officers were indicted, the 1986 Computer Fraud and Abuse Act draws no distinction between the unauthorized intrusion into commercial systems as opposed to that into national security systems. Thus, the U.S. legal basis for, say, indicting other PLA officers for breaking into Pentagon computers would have been no different.

[43] U.S. Department of Justice, Office of Public Affairs, "U.S. Charges Five Chinese Military Hackers for Cyber Espionage Against U.S. Corporations and a Labor Organization for Commercial Advantage," Washington, D.C., May 19, 2014.

- from ATI: information on network credentials, probably associated with a joint venture and with a trade dispute with a Chinese state-owned enterprise
- from Alcoa: emails, including internal discussions about a partnership with a Chinese state-owned enterprise
- from the United Steelworkers: e-mails associated with strategies related to pending trade disputes.

Note that every single organization that was hacked was dealing with the Chinese either as a business partner or as a commercial disputant. With the exception of a reference to the "manufacturing methods" of Solar World,[44] there were very few indications of intellectual property theft.[45]

China took immediate umbrage at the indictments and withdrew from the Track One Cyber Working Group talks that had been initiated the year before. Its irritation was hardly assuaged with the promulgation of an Executive Order on April 1, 2015: "Blocking the Property of Certain Persons Engaging in Significant Malicious Cyber-Enabled Activities."[46]

---

[44] The information on piping associated with Westinghouse piping might indicate intellectual property, but it might have been taken in a Chinese effort to understand the cost basis for Westinghouse's bid and thereby find a more advantageous price to offer for Westinghouse's services.

[45] Perhaps U.S. government officials believe that revealing intellectual property theft would be more harmful than revealing the theft of proprietary business information (although how that choice would survive the discovery process if the indictments actually went to trial is unclear). There have been proposals to treat EMCE as a trade issue. China has signed the Trade-Related Aspects of Intellectual Property Rights (TRIPS) agreement under the World Trade Organization. TRIPS enjoins countries from stealing intellectual property but is less clear about profiting from the theft of business proprietary data. If the Chinese really are interested more in the latter, the case that their action violated TRIPS is correspondingly harder to make.

[46] See Barack Obama, "Executive Order—'Blocking the Property of Certain Persons Engaging in Significant Malicious Cyber-Enabled Activities,'" Washington, D.C.: The White House, April 1, 2015. The Chinese seemed to take the order as aimed at them, although it also seemed to reflect U.S. sanctions on certain North Koreans following the Sony hack.

Track Two Talks Between CICIR and CSIS

In 2009, seeking to counter growing U.S. complaints over cyber espionage, China proposed opening up Track Two negotiations on cyberspace with a group of prominent U.S. counterparts.[47] The Chinese side was staffed by CICIR; its delegations have included a growing number of government officials over time. The U.S. side was headed by CSIS but drew participants from across the Washington, D.C., think-tank community, as well as, over time, an expanding cohort of government officials, to the point that it may be more accurate to view the dialogue as a Track 1.5, or mixed official-unofficial meeting. As of this writing, nine sessions of dialogue have taken place, starting in December 2009 in Washington, D.C., and alternating between spring and summer in Beijing and early winter in Washington. The eighth meeting (May 2013) was followed by a hiatus because of the beginning and termination of the Track One talks between the two countries. A ninth meeting took place in Washington in February 2015.

Collectively, the nine sessions were marked more by continuity than change—for the most part, the positions that the U.S. and Chinese interlocutors came in with six years ago are those that they continue to give voice to today. Among the changes that have been observed on the Chinese side is the decreasing concern that they cannot cope with the challenge that the Internet has posed to Chinese society. Correspondingly, China rarely links its complaints about alleged U.S. support of dissident material on the Internet to U.S. complaints about unwelcome Chinese activities in cyberspace. The Chinese emphasis on sovereignty in the information sphere persisted throughout the engagements. Another major theme throughout was China's perception that the United States dominated and would continue to dominate cyberspace and that the United States therefore had less to worry about in

---

[47] With the Russians, the United States has entertained more formal negotiations, one product of which has been an agreement on a "hotline" in cyberspace, so that incidents potentially involving both countries can be talked over before they become full-fledged crises. Faster progress with Russia (at least until 2014) may have benefited from over 50 years of formal bilateral negotiations, resulting in a well-worn sense of how to deal with each other. Such history has yet to be made with China.

that domain than everyone else. China's view is that, as a consequence of this position enjoyed by the United States, its complaints about cyberattacks were groundless. Chinese representatives cited numerous ways in which their country was dependent on U.S. capabilities: Their credit card and airline reservations systems were housed in the United States; their emergency communications depended on a U.S. corporation; their offices depended on Microsoft, whose actions in 2008 (when an upgrade made many Chinese screens go dark[48]) and 2012 (when it persuaded a U.S. court to shut down a Chinese website, 3322.org) were not forgotten. China participants expressed a conviction that companies, such as Microsoft, were scooping up vast quantities of personal data on China's netizens and that this information could be subpoenaed or otherwise transferred to the U.S. government.

The Chinese participants in these discussions were acutely conscious of China's difficulties in keeping the Internet running both in the face of glitches (one noted that 17 provinces, at one point or another, lost Domain Name System services) and the "fact" that the United States controlled all the top-level domains (.gov, .org, .com, and .edu, etc.).[49] China saw no basis for U.S. concerns about supply chain security, except as a guide to how they might, themselves, manage the risk.

The Chinese participants were also alarmed by Stuxnet (at least in its immediate aftermath) and the formation of USCYBERCOM, which they argued was proof that the United States wanted to militarize cyberspace, while the lack of an announced Chinese counterpart was pointed to as proof of China's peaceful intentions. Such suspicion extended to their (now-abandoned) perception that the Department of Homeland Security's Cyber Storm exercises were preparations for hunkering down in the face of a U.S.-sponsored cyberwar.[50] There was

---

[48] Thomas Claburn, "Chinese Hackers Angered by Microsoft's Epic Fail," *Information Week*, October 23, 2008.

[49] China conflates the headquartering of these domains in the United States with the domains being controlled by the U.S. government.

[50] U.S. Department of Homeland Security, "Cyber Storm: Securing Cyberspace," Web page, December 1, 2015.

similar suspicion over the United States arrogating the right to respond to a cyberattack, in large part because China did not trust U.S. attribution claims, since the Chinese themselves could not do attribution very well, although they clearly wanted to improve their own capabilities in this area.

The Chinese have tended to view the problem of cyberwar from an arms-control perspective, asking such questions as, "What is a cyberweapon?" "Should weapons that cannot distinguish between military and civilian targets be banned?" and "Is there any way to create a cyberspace equivalent of *taggants* (a marker embedded in explosive chemicals that identifies them by source or point of origin)?"

Finally, although the Chinese understood the U.S. disquiet about China's EMCE, they refused to address whether EMCE was or was not legitimate in a world in which national-security cyber espionage was considered something that countries now routinely do. Many participants in the dialogue have spoken of the need for mutual trust, arguing that the United States must show that it considers China trustworthy and act correspondingly, and have argued that China should not be accused of cybercrimes.[51]

---

[51] The notion of *mutual trust*, so often repeated by Chinese analysts across a wide variety of contexts, is often confusing to American observers. According to Qian Yingyi, Jia Qingguo, Bai Chong'en, and Wang Jisi, *mutual strategic trust*, in U.S.-China relations, means that both sides are aware of each other's strategic purposes while holding positive expectations of each other's positions and actions on issues of vital interests. Building mutual strategic trust does not mean China and the United States deny that conflicts of interest and ideological differences exist between them. On the contrary, it means that both sides would strive to reduce the impact of conflicts and differences on bilateral relationships and form long-term healthy interactions based on an agreement that they share more common interests than differences. See Qian Yingyi, Jia Qingguo, Bai Chong'en, and Wang Jisi, "Building Mutual Trust Between China and the U.S.," in Shao Binhong, ed., *The World in 2020 According to China: Chinese Foreign Policy Elites Discuss Emerging Trends in International Politics*, Leiden, The Netherlands: Koninklijke Brill NV, 2014, pp. 277–291.

What Could the United States Do to Discourage China's EMCE?

China's public response to the various accusations of having carried out cyber espionage has been flat denial.[52] Remarks by Qian Xiaoqian, vice minister and deputy director of the State Internet Information Office, are broadly representative of China's position when charged with cyber espionage:

> Our opposition to all forms of hacking is clear and consistent . . . Lately people have been cooking up a theory of a Chinese Internet threat, which is just an extension of the old "China threat" and just as groundless.[53]

Furthermore, many Chinese say they believe that the United States carries out EMCE, even if they have no specific evidence to point to, and Chinese officials add that China is itself a victim of cybercrime emanating from the United States. More recently, China has called accusations that it had hacked the OPM,

> groundless accusations [that] would surely harm mutual trust between the two big powers of today's world [generated] . . . without any proof [inasmuch as] . . . cyberattacks, usually conducted anonymously and across borders, are hard to trace back.[54]

Absent a change in Chinese views about the credibility of claims about attribution, getting China to admit its involvement in any instance of cyber espionage is likely to be impossible, regardless of how often U.S. officials demand confessions, apologies, or changes in the behavior of their Chinese counterparts.

---

[52] "Admit Nothing and Deny Everything," *The Economist*, June 8, 2013.

[53] See Christopher Bodeen, "U.S. Says Hacking Undermines China's Interests," *Pioneer Press*, April 9, 2013. See also "Official Urges China-U.S. Trust on Cyber Security," Xinhua, April 10, 2013.

[54] For instance Zhu Junqing, "Commentary: U.S. Wronging of China for Cyber Breaches Harm Mutual Trust," Xinhua, June 6, 2015.

Suppose that the United States were prepared to do more than talk (or indict individuals who are highly unlikely to present themselves for trial). What would the United States ask China to do? How likely is it that the United States would succeed? What risks would be run in trying (or succeeding)?

If the United States could establish norms that would distinguish EMCE from its national-security counterpart, it would have to concede that much of what concerns the United States about China's cyber espionage (such as its penetration of OPM) is no less legitimate than U.S. cyber espionage inasmuch as it is aimed at traditional state targets. Similarly, China's purported penetration of Lockheed Martin's F-35 production works,[55] its attack on RSA (to penetrate such targets as Lockheed Martin), and its earlier intrusions into U.S. government agencies might all fall within a broad-scope definition of forms of espionage dedicated to national security that the United States sees as legitimate (if, to be sure, undesirable when it finds itself and its defense-industrial sector the target).

One challenge is that what constitutes national security for China may not necessarily be viewed the same in the United States. China apparently carried out cyber espionage against the *New York Times* because one of its reporters wrote about the family of then–Prime Minister Wen Jiabao amassing an enormous amount of unexplained wealth.[56] To a country that fears popular agitation over official corruption, such charges might constitute a national security concern; to the United States with its First Amendment, it is not a legitimate national security concern.[57]

Another barrier to eliminating Chinese EMCE might be that the Chinese believe that the size and scope of potential gains might out-

---

[55] Gorman, Cole, and Dreazen, 2009.

[56] Nicole Perlroth, "Hackers in China Attacked the Times for Last Four Months," *New York Times*, January 31, 2013.

[57] China treats anything that reflects poorly on the reputation of the ruling party as a threat to the stability of the regime, hence a matter of national security. The United States does not regard such an approach to political speech as legitimate or in conformity with international human rights norms.

weigh the penalties the United States might seek to impose on China for continuing to carry out EMCE. There could be a future in which both the United States and China conclude that both sides would be better off if neither carried out EMCE. Each country then would not need to spend so much on cyber defense, and the returns for the effort to generate intellectual property would be higher, since both sides would get unique possession of what they had generated (in some cases, invented). One could imagine a deal making both the United States and China better off. That being so, there is no settlement (or, as economists would understand it, *set of side payments*) that would make both sides better off. This means that a resolution requires confrontation, in which the United States tries to get China to abandon its EMCE or face consequences. Hence, the current strategy (as of this writing) is diplomatic nagging with modest consequences.

Implicit in these confrontations is that the continuation of EMCE will imperil U.S. friendship, which the U.S. government would have to presume is worth more to the Chinese than what the Chinese gain from EMCE. Presumably, the cost to the United States of severing its friendship with China is that China does likewise. Ultimately, the question is of power: which country needs the other more? One Chinese delegate to the ninth CSIS-CICIR talks remarked that the United States, by virtue of its power and position, is the only country that cannot be (effectively) sanctioned. How long this remains true in the face of economic and other trends remains to be seen.

CHAPTER FOUR
Getting to Yes?

To further explore the options for advancing cooperation and minimizing distrust with China over issues of cybersecurity, we conducted a series of meetings in Beijing with officials from government agencies tasked with managing the cyber issue, current and retired PLA officers who focus on cybersecurity, experts from government think tanks, and academic specialists. Our interviews were semistructured in the sense that we had a few consistent questions: What would it take to restart negotiations (suspended at the time of our discussions)? What could such negotiations accomplish? What would be required to sustain the momentum of such talks? And what would the Chinese like to see from the United States in these negotiations? These questions were lead-ins to a broader discussion (in a few cases, our interlocutors spoke first). This chapter reflects our findings and what these conversations revealed about how the United States might move toward greater cooperation with China over cyberspace.

Setting

The U.S.-China disagreement over each other's actions in cyberspace is asymmetric in terms of issues of concern and prioritization. The United States would like China to stop its intrusions into the networks of commercial companies; the Chinese just want the issue to go away. Reflecting this difference in priorities, one interviewee we spoke with, an expert on the U.S.-China relationship, observed that, while cyberspace was within the top five issues of concern in the United States, it probably did not even rank among China's top ten issues. Another noted that he had never seen an issue rise to the top of the U.S.-China bilateral policy discussion agenda as rapidly as cyberspace has, something that a third observer commented appeared to have caught the Chinese leadership somewhat by surprise. A fourth interlocutor commented that, although both sides were conscious of the fragility of key infrastructures, such concerns were expressed far more frequently and vociferously in the United States.

Chinese interlocutors recognize that the cyber issue is an irritant in relations between the two countries and that it erodes strategic trust (as the Chinese put it). A reduction in strategic trust, in turn, may complicate the resolution of other issues (e.g., trade, environment, geostrategic matters). It may also increase the odds of future conflict, either accidental or intentional. Thus, even if one believes that little in cyberspace makes much difference compared with controversies in the physical world (e.g., South China Sea), resolving issues in that medium could have a knock-on effect outside it and vice versa.

As noted, the United States has at least three cyberspace-related issues with China: its EMCE, its potential threat to the U.S. critical infrastructure, and the mutual risk of strategic misunderstanding. They would seem to call for negotiations, mutual assurance, and mutual understanding, respectively.

We start with our assessment of the negotiation climate and proceed to the possible areas for negotiation.

Track One Negotiations

In keeping with past official and unofficial statements, our Chinese interlocutors frequently and sometimes forcefully asserted that Track One negotiations could not restart as long as the five PLA members are still under indictment. Many of our interlocutors appeared to be genuinely outraged that the United States had indicted Chinese military officers for hacking. One high-level interlocutor we spoke with suggested that, to move forward, "the United States should get down on its knees and beg for forgiveness like [former German Prime Minister]

Willy Brandt," stating that "this would win points with the Chinese people."[1] Another high-level interlocutor argued at length that this indictment was quite contrary to international law and practice, since cyber espionage could not be in any way construed as a war crime. Chinese interlocutors repeatedly expressed an interest in whether or not the indictments could be retracted or quashed.[2]

If it is difficult to imagine China returning to Track One negotiations without a resolution of the indictments, it is even more difficult to imagine the United States dropping the indictments just because China asks it to do so.[3] Still, after having made their representations on the unjustified nature of the indictments, some interlocutors at government and military-linked think tanks did suggest that there might be a way to resume formal negotiations even if the United States refuses to drop the indictments. One of the ideas suggested by our interlocutors was to simply set up a new formal dialogue mechanism on cyber, calling it something other than the Cyber Working Group and locating it in a different forum than the Strategic Security Dialogue within the S&ED. One respondent thought that shifting the locus of the discussion from the U.S.-China S&ED to another forum would permit talks to restart without contravening China's determination not to halt talks until the indictments are resolved. Since such a new dialogue mechanism is unrelated to the PLA indictment, it could proceed without needing to await resolution of that case.

However, we have found considerable sentiment in China that Track One negotiations are not doing much more than providing each side another opportunity to present its point of view to the other. Two high-level interlocutors concluded that the best approach under current circumstances would be to convene a standing or continuous (as opposed to a biannual) working group. Such a working group could serve multiple purposes: to work out proposals (some of which would require considerable technical input) prior to any formal negotiations

---

[1]   Interview in Beijing, 2015.

[2]   Interview in Beijing, 2015.

[3]   A few respondents felt similarly about the executive order (Obama, 2015). To wit, it was aimed at China, definitely hostile, and a barrier to the resumption of talks.

by the two sides, to produce a combined set of norms of conduct in cyberspace to replace the Tallinn manual and the joint China-Russian cyber declaration issued through the Shanghai Cooperation Organization (SCO), or even to look into claims of hacking from either side and reach a joint evaluation of their merit and assign attribution.[4]

Unofficial negotiations can be a means of developing ideas, particularly those that depend on whether some technology will do what it claims or whether some policy will achieve the hoped-for goals. Compliance verification, for instance, can be very tricky in cyberspace, even trickier perhaps than it is in the physical world (e.g., to oversee another country's nuclear program). These issues cannot be worked exclusively in periodic formal dialogue. But the notion that informal groups will generate something that governments will agree to by acclamation is equally implausible. All informal negotiations over cybersecurity must, at some point, return to Track One if they are to achieve concrete and lasting impact.

Many respondents brought up the importance of developing either a memorandum of understanding or a set of confidence-building measures (CBMs), expressing the hope—since realized—that such deals might be signed or announced during the September 2015 summit. There appeared to be more emphasis on doing something that could signify the capacity for China and the United States to get along rather than striving to accomplish anything specific by that date.

Economically Motivated Cyber Espionage

China's official position on U.S. accusations that China carries out EMCE is an unequivocal denial, coupled with assertions that accurate and definitive attribution is essentially impossible in cyberspace.[5] Several of our interlocutors maintained that Chinese-based Internet

---

[4] One difficulty, however, may be that the SCO document refers to peacetime behavior, and the Tallinn manual refers to wartime behavior.

[5] Some U.S. subject-matter experts we spoke with, however, expressed the view that Chinese expressions of doubt over the possibility of attribution are little more than talking points, arguing that the Chinese side knows attribution is not only possible but, in many cases, is not even all that difficult, given the sloppy nature of a number of Chinese cyber intrusions. Interviews with U.S. cybersecurity experts, Washington, D.C., June 2015.

Protocol (IP) addresses associated with incoming attacks prove nothing about who is carrying them out and that such accusations reflect an anti-China narrative. As recently as early 2015, according to at least one respondent, this was personally reiterated by President Xi.[6]

Thus, it was a surprise to us that only one of our interlocutors, a high-level respondent, voiced a flat-out denial that China was carrying out EMCE;[7] two respondents even seemed to tacitly admit that EMCE was taking place by arguing that U.S. claims that IP theft accounted for China's economic growth were grossly overstated. Several others talked in general terms about the difficulty of attribution, but many of those who did so had China's difficulty of doing attribution in mind (several mentioned explicitly how badly China was doing it), while others were talking about attribution in general. Conversely, when we noted to them that the United States took issue with EMCE originating from China, there was no pushback (apart from the aforementioned high-level interlocutor). No one claimed that the United States itself was carrying out EMCE.

A related question is whether our Chinese respondents viewed EMCE as less legitimate than cyber espionage carried out for more traditional national-security purposes. In the interviews, we explained the U.S. position: to wit, that the United States found EMCE particularly obnoxious and wanted China to stop conducting it. Most respondents chose not to contest the statement; a couple even seemed to agree with the sentiment. However, one high-level interlocutor completely disagreed, arguing that cyber espionage for national-security purposes was less desirable than EMCE.

In fairness, the proposition that EMCE is less legitimate than national-security cyber espionage does not derive from international law and does not constitute a universally accepted proposition. While the United States does not engage in EMCE, China is not the only

---

[6]   Interview in Beijing, May 2015.

[7]   Unfortunately, that respondent was most inclined to agree with the U.S. position that EMCE was less legitimate than national-security cyber espionage.

country that seems to regard it as a legitimate form of espionage.[8] No other country has been the target of EMCE complaints to the extent that China has, however. Furthermore, the United States has not specifically complained about other countries' EMCE to the degree that it has cited China for such behavior. China, for its part, may view EMCE as a particularly attractive and legitimate form of espionage because of the closely intertwined nature of the Chinese state and economy. Thus, distinguishing espionage on public targets (legitimate) from espionage on private targets (illegitimate) accords more closely with the U.S. political-economic system than it does with China's.

What Does China Want?

We now ask the question: What would China want from the United States in exchange for an agreement to establish certain norms in cyberspace, most prominently a meaningful and enforceable norm against EMCE?

Interestingly, almost all of our interlocutors struggled to identify anything specific or substantial that they thought China wants as a concession from the United States in negotiations over cybersecurity. Nor did we get the impression that their inability to articulate a set of demands was because they had a list whose priority rankings they were still working on or even a set of requests whose value they were still trying to measure. They simply seemed to have no specific ask.

Our interlocutors provided general responses to this question. Some bemoaned the lack of mutual trust between China and the United States; they clearly implied (and sometimes asserted) that things would be much better if the United States trusted China more. Several respondents indicated that they would like the United States to stop criticizing the Chinese for carrying out EMCE—which U.S. officials would, no doubt, agree to in exchange for there not being

---

[8] The U.S. position prior to the Edward Snowden revelations was that *all* cyber espionage was carried out in pursuit of national security. After Snowden, the claim is that the United States does not carry out EMCE and deliver the results to U.S. corporations to enhance their competitiveness. This claim is credible insofar as providing such results preferentially to one corporation but not another is fundamentally incompatible with how the United States treats specific private enterprises.

any EMCE to criticize.[9] Others wanted the United States to foreswear criticizing China over its human rights policies or, more specifically, to suppress websites that broadcast messages contrary to the interests or ruling status of the CPC. Neither proposition is compatible with the First Amendment. The interlocutors also appeared to place great stock in getting the broad picture right, on the assumption that the details would follow: One respondent, for example, thought that, if the two countries could agree to trust each other more, a meeting of the minds on North Korean hacking would naturally follow. He added that mutual restraint was a matter of successively controlling intent, then activity, and last weapons (U.S. officials might well reverse that order).[10]

When specific requests were mentioned, they were usually speculative or were of relatively low importance to China. For instance, requests included "stop funding Internet censorship circumvention technologies," something the United States dedicates just a few million dollars to every year.[11] Another request, "stop blocking U.S. market access for Huawei and ZTE," seemed not to reflect a realistic understanding of what the United States might be willing to do.[12] Some noted that China does not want technology transfer to suffer under a presumption of suspicion and denial and hoped that the United States might lift prohibitions on transfer of advanced technologies to China.[13]

Other propositions suggested by other respondents were less unreasonable, but it is not clear that the propositions can become the basis of a deal. Several of the other respondents mentioned their dis-

---

[9] U.S. officials would have to stop leaking information to the press that China did it in those cases when the neutral body indicates either that China did not do it (and perhaps even when it cannot come to a conclusion). This is not altogether as obvious as it sounds. Were there a serious agreement, U.S. officials might have to modulate its public behavior when attribution was short of ironclad.

[10] Interview in Beijing, May 2015.

[11] Nicole Gaouette, and Brendan Greeley, "U.S. Funds Help Democracy Activists Evade Internet Crackdowns," Bloomberg, April 20, 2011

[12] Interview in Beijing, May 2015.

[13] IBM was criticized for its offer to transfer technology to China. See David Wolf, "Why Buy the Hardware When China Is Getting the IP for Free?" *Foreign Policy*, April 24, 2015.

like of U.S. leadership of ICANN and the fact that ten of the top-level domain–root name servers are based in the United States (the other three are in Sweden, Japan, and the Netherlands). Some respondents opined that the rest of the world in general, and China in particular, should have more say in the Internet. Granted, the issue of Internet governance has been contentious, but it is rarely linked directly to cybersecurity concerns. The official U.S. position is that, under U.S. aegis, the Internet has expanded very quickly and serves the needs of all nations. The system is not broken (and our respondents adduced no particular faults that required broader representation to correct, nor were they able to say what harm the current system poses to Chinese interests other than the absence of prestige that China appears to associate with the hosting of such servers); therefore, there is no reason to fix it in the U.S. view.

Furthermore, another clear candidate for Internet governance— the International Telecommunications Union (ITU), now under the UN—would introduce many potentially harmful features into Internet governance. While the Internet was and, to some extent, still is a creature of and for engineers eager for innovation, the ITU represents governments and state-owned phone companies, some quite wary of innovation. The Internet represents the triumph of end-to-end engineering principles; it comprises a relatively simple core coupled with intelligent peripheral devices. The ITU, on the other hand, is more familiar with phone-company architectures of complex cores and simple peripheral devices. The Internet, famously, is routed around censorship. Many UN member governments practice censorship, and the United States government (as well as U.S. high-technology companies) does not want to see an Internet made safe for censorship and surveillance. It is unclear why China, which does not need to change international governance of the Internet to maintain censorship on its end, would view this as a high-priority issue. Overall, we do not see reasons to believe that either side would trade restrictions on cyber espionage for changes in Internet governance, if for no other reason than because the first is a bilateral issue, while the latter is a multilateral issue.

Surprisingly, despite the apparent confidence that China has about the accuracy of the Snowden leaks regarding the breadth and the depth of NSA penetration into Chinese networks, our interlocutors exhibited little interest in seeking to restrain U.S. cyber espionage against them in exchange for Chinese restraint on EMCE. We cannot be certain about the reason, but one implication is clear: It is unlikely that there will be an agreement in which the United States can trade espionage-related concession to China to obtain relief from Chinese EMCE. The notion of making a trade over behaviors in cyberspace requires China to admit to having engaged in EMCE (something it has yet to acknowledge it does) and problematically suggests that compliance with such a norm would be driven less by any sense of what behavior is legitimate and illegitimate and more by a transactional logic (giving lip service in hopes of getting something in return).

Among those we talked to, there was a strong sense that the United States should be the one to make concessions because it is more powerful than China in cyberspace. The contrast between this posture and the U.S. demands that China stop what the United States considers unlawful behavior is consistent with Chapter Two's discussion. To wit, the Chinese focus on power and the U.S. focuses on law (and unlawful activity) as a basis for international relations.

Alternatives to Bilateral Negotiations with China

Several respondents and high-level interlocutors asked us specifically about whether or not the Internet principles endorsed by the SCO could serve as a basis for international norms of behavior in cyberspace.[14] The United States has refused to endorse these principles, notably because of their emphasis on state sovereignty at the expense of Internet freedom. But even if these principles were consistent with U.S. values, there is considerable doubt within the United States that general principles, as such, are good substitutes for more specific guidelines about what countries can and cannot do in cyberspace. The U.S. ten-

---

[14] The SCO members are China, Russia, Kazakhstan, Kyrgyzstan, Tajikistan, and Uzbekistan.

dency is to build principles up from practice, while China's tendency appears to work in reverse order.

The broader but unresolved issue is whether multilateral agreements on state norms of behavior in cyberspace can adequately address issues that divide the United States and China, bearing in mind that the resolution of bilateral issues is of greater importance to the United States—while maintaining a positive bilateral relationship appears, so far, to be of greater importance to China. The United States is not opposed to multilateral negotiations over cybersecurity; it has participated in the UN Group of Government Experts to win international consensus that the Law of Armed Conflict (LOAC) applies to cyberspace just as much as they do in the physical world.[15]

Multilateral agreements have several advantages over bilateral agreements. They tend to assume a more permanent rather than ad hoc status. Furthermore, they can address the deeds of many rather than the deeds of one. For example, until recently, the term *advanced persistent threat* was used in the United States almost exclusively to refer to Chinese hacking groups. Since the Russo-Ukrainian conflict broke out, however, Russia has increasingly demonstrated an ability and willingness to conduct similarly sophisticated and long-term intrusive cyber espionage operations.[16] Thus, it is illusory to believe that an end to China's EMCE also means an end to troubling intrusions into even private networks.

But bilateral agreements have their own rationale. Meaningful agreements are easier to make—one Chinese respondent claimed that Russia would play the spoiler in any multilateral negotiation.[17] If the United States is part of the talks, many of its allies can be expected to fall in line behind whatever the United States agrees to in cyberspace.

---

[15] Alex Grigsby, "The UN GGE on Cybersecurity: What is the UN's Role?" Council on Foreign Relations (Net Politics blog), April 15, 2015.

[16] The Russians have been continually active in cyber espionage, but their tradecraft was good enough to mask the full extent of their activity. Newfound indicators of their activity may show (1) more aggressive activity, (2) a certain slipping of their tradecraft standards so as to advertise their prowess, or (3) both.

[17] Interview in Beijing, 2015.

Furthermore, it is easier to generate explicit trades in bilateral talks than it is in multilateral talks, where such trades tend to require that participants separate themselves into two camps before each can know whether its offers would be reciprocated. Finally, if the whole point of the negotiations is to remove obstacles to better U.S.-China relations, a bilateral agreement is a must. More to the point, if the United States requires that China stop its EMCE to gain strategic trust from the United States, it is hard to see how this could be achieved within a multilateral forum.

A related issue is whether the larger problems between the United States and China can be addressed by starting with CBMs in the hope that the mutual strategic trust gained can be used to lubricate agreement on these larger issues. Confidence building takes time: to find appropriate measures, to ensure that each side is behaving in a trustworthy fashion, and to learn from that experience. One of the potential costs of adopting a CBM-based approach is that the effort to work through issues and build up a set of solutions to lesser problems may delay addressing the more important disagreements that divide the two sides. However, if the United States and China opt to move forward through a focus on CBMs, potential areas of shared interest include combatting spam, child pornography, non–state-sponsored cybercrime, and terrorist recruiting. Additionally, Chinese respondents advocated enhanced information sharing; more cooperation between the Federal Bureau of Investigation and China's Ministry of Public Security (which means placing more emphasis on solving crimes whose victims are in the other country); more cooperation among each side's computer emergency response teams, an approach that also means paying more attention to issues brought up by the other government; and sharing information on how to use private lawsuits to protect intellectual property.[18]

---

[18] U.S. efforts to teach China about the public court system have run into problems with the Chinese government, which sees efforts to promote the rule of law as undermining its authority. It would appear that civil justice would not implicate these authority issues and could be presented as a fillip to the formation of Chinese high-technology startups.

The last issue is whether negotiations should take place synchronously (as is the usual custom) or asynchronously. The asynchronous approach consists of virtuous circles started when one side makes a unilateral gesture or concession, the other side reciprocates, and the first side in turn offers something else.[19]

The primary advantage of an asynchronous strategy of reciprocity is that each side can pretend that its offers are entirely gratuitous, not made in exchange for anything, and merely symptomatic of its high regard for the other side and its overall dedication to fairness. The disadvantage, in this particular case, is that it offers no option for verification, since the steps are not explicitly acknowledged to be in relation to one another or conditional on the other side's actions. Nor can an asynchronous approach lead to the building of institutions (e.g., a bilateral verification effort). Not surprisingly, China feels that, because the United States is superior in cyberspace, it should make the first move (and probably several moves after that as well, given the perceived superiority in overall power terms of the United States vis-à-vis China).

The Law of Armed Conflict and the Right to Retaliate

One of the issues that we explored in our discussions with Chinese interlocutors was their view of the applicability to cyberspace of laws and norms, such as the LOAC, or the right to retaliate following an attack. As noted above, while the United States has an interest in a common understanding that cyberwar should come under LOAC, China is uncomfortable with the notion. In theory, putting cyberwar under LOAC subjects this activity to more restrictions (e.g., avoid targeting purely civilian systems), but China argues that the key effect of

---

[19] This approach was made famous through the game theoretic work of Robert Axelrod's studies of the tit-for-tat strategy in computerized game play of the Prisoner's Dilemma in Robert Axelrod, *The Evolution of Cooperation*, New York: Basic Books, 1984. It is also recommended in Lyle J. Goldstein, *Meeting China Halfway*, Washington, D.C.: Georgetown University Press, 2015, although Goldstein does not discuss applying such an approach to relations with China over cybersecurity.

putting cyberwar under LOAC is not to place limits on cyberwar, but to legitimize it as a concept and to militarize cyberspace.[20]

Chinese interlocutors were especially uncomfortable with the U.S. assertion of a unilateral right to respond to cyberattacks. A number of respondents mentioned the U.S. Department of Defense's (DoD's) cyber strategy with alarm: one labeled it the "pursuit of unilateral power."[21] They were anxious to know to what extent it represented a departure from the White House's 2011 *International Strategy for Cyberspace: Prosperity, Security, and Openness in a Networked World.*[22] Indeed, while seeing the latter as troubling, interlocutors preferred it to DoD's document, imbuing the White House strategy with a patina of reasonableness (something not characteristic of China's statements about the same document when it was first issued in 2011).[23]

When we probed the question of the right to retaliate for a cyberattack, all of our Chinese respondents were reluctant to say how China would respond to a hypothetical scenario in which one of its (unnamed) neighbors had hacked into a Chinese government–run media outlet and thereby shut down operations and destroyed computers. A typical response was that cyberattacks are not physical attacks and that having suffered a cyberattack would not be grounds to declare a state of war. If kinetic conflict in the physical world was not already ongoing, countries should not respond to a cyberattack with hostile actions of their own. It was hard for our respondents to imagine a cyberattack

---

[20] This finding is consistent with the experiences of other researchers. For example, Ashley Deeks reports that Professor Huang Zhixiong of Wuhan University criticized the Tallinn Manual for adopting too low a bar on what constitutes a use of force in cyberspace, argued against states' rights to invoke the right of self-defense, proclaimed that states do not have the right to carry out self-defense attacks against nonstate actors or engage in preemptive cyber-attack, and stated that we should generally not be thinking about the ways in which the International LOAC could be applied to cyberspace. See Deeks, 2015.

[21] U.S. Department of Defense, *The Department of Defense Cyber Strategy,* April 2015.

[22] White House, 2011.

[23] It is unclear whether the difference between the documents represents a shift in U.S. deterrence strategy (particularly after North Korea's cyberattacks on Sony) or whether it reflects the fact that the first one emerged from the interagency process (and was thus carefully hedged), while the second one was a product solely of DoD. Our respondents did not appear convinced that the latter was the case when it was explained thusly.

that could create damage tantamount to that of war. This probably should not be interpreted to suggest that China would never respond to a cyberattack but that Chinese thinkers have yet to seriously grapple with this issue. Therefore, they have not yet specifically considered the kinds of attacks they would respond to or how.

In light of the aforementioned analysis of China's deterrence thinking, the Chinese respondents' responses would likely take into account the overall relationship between China and the perceived source of the cyberattack, including not only an assessment of what sort of force was used and what damage was caused but also the domestic political implications of the attack (is the Chinese government under public pressure to show its response, or is knowledge of the attacks limited to a select circle of policy elites?) and the Chinese government's assessment of its ability to come out ahead by responding. In short, China's response would likely depend on far more than an assessment of the impact of a cyberattack.

We interpreted these reactions as evidence that China does not yet have an explicit cyber-deterrence posture. The classic notion of deterrence has four prerequisites: thresholds, attribution, credibility, and capability (to respond). Furthermore, an effective deterrence policy requires that these prerequisites be met in the view of potential attackers. For example, even if the target thinks it has a capability to attribute, if the potential attacker thinks that the target of the attack lacks confidence in its own attribution, deterrence suffers. If the Chinese had a serious cyber-deterrence posture, the rest of world would not have to guess what it is; it would know.

Note that this is different from saying that China's cyber-deterrence posture is simply reflective of China's overall deterrence posture. Overall, China maintains a substantial degree of ambiguity as a strategy to magnify its influence and ability to compel respect. Nonetheless, China has made clear that its "forbearance has limits"[24]—it simply declines to specify their exact location, instead favoring an approach of hinting at

---

[24] Paul H. B. Godwin and Alice L. Miller, *China's Forbearance Has Limits: Chinese Threat and Retaliation Signaling and Its Implications for a Sino-American Military Confrontation*, Washington, D.C.: National Defense University Press, April 2013.

direction and proximity and allowing the target of deterrence to infer that it is running increasing risks of a kinetic Chinese reaction. In the cyber domain, in contrast, China has not clarified to any meaningful extent its ability to detect actions that cross its (unstated) red lines, declaims a nigh-absolute degree of doubt about the possibility of attribution in cyberspace, and has expressed no clear statement about its own willingness to respond to cyberattacks. Indeed, China has gone far as to lay down somewhat costly markers that it may have to walk back from if it ever decides that it does want to respond to a cyberattack either through a cyber or kinetic response.

As noted earlier, if China doubts its ability to definitively attribute an attack but perceives an intrusion as having originated from the United States, it will have to carefully weigh several factors in its response, such as weighing its its lack of confidence in its own attribution capabilities and its weaker power vis-à-vis the United States against its concerns that U.S. actions might be oriented toward affecting a qualitative change in the overall balance of power. Additionally, CPC leaders would have to consider any possible consequences for domestic regime stability. Several additional considerations are likely to shape China's cyber-deterrence posture:

- China's leaders are acutely aware of the vulnerable state of the country's network infrastructure.
- Compared with the everyday risks to China's infrastructure (entire provinces have been knocked offline because of the misadventures of computer games),[25] risks originating from overseas may appear less pressing than they do in the United States.
- At the same time, if China is perceived to have suffered a cyberattack, the political pressures that the CPC leadership may find themselves under could be equal to or even greater than those that the United States experiences, since the regime depends more heavily on nationalism and because the risks to any leader for not acting could imperil his or her own position (since authority is

---

[25] Owen Fletcher, "China Game Boss Sniped Rivals, Took Down Internet," *PC World*, August 29, 2009.

more personalized and less institutionalized in China than in the United States).[26]

- China's perspective on deterrence is more holistic than the U.S. perspective (as argued in Chapter Two).
- China lags the United States in cyberspace policymaking in terms of high-level statements, publicly issued documents, and the establishment of policy decisionmaking organs.

Overall, those respondents who ventured an opinion on the matter believed the United States was far ahead of China in terms of its cyberwar capability.[27] One believed that China was catching up. Two respondents voiced fears that the United States would target China's nuclear command-and-control infrastructure.[28]

A Mutual Forbearance Proposal

Our U.S. colleagues who had experience interviewing subjects about cybersecurity in China advised us not to expect our Chinese interlocutors to offer much in the way of negotiating initiatives. Given this knowledge, we decided to suggest some ourselves and gauge our interlocutors' reactions to them.[29] Accordingly, we presented the following three-part proposal to our Chinese interviewees for their consideration and reaction.

---

[26] One possible counter to this is that the Chinese side controls the media to a much higher degree than the United States does and, in the absence of muckraking journalism, stories about cyberattacks on China almost never make it into the Chinese news media because the government prefers to keep these quiet.

[27] Interview in Beijing, May 2015.

[28] Interviews in Beijing, May 2015. We put a comment about Chinese inferences from Stuxnet in that category, even though Stuxnet targeted a nuclear production facility, not nuclear command and control.

[29] Prior to conducting our research trip, we convened a two-hour roundtable discussion with five prominent U.S. subject-matter experts on Chinese views of cybersecurity and took their advice and reactions to our planned interview questionnaire. We are grateful to the individuals who participated in this discussion, which assisted us in refining our interview questions before we traveled to China.

Given that the United States and China would like to reduce mutual suspicion in cyberspace, one option might be the negotiation of agreement on a set of norms. Since both sides express concern over the possibility of the other side targeting its critical infrastructure, the core of the deal would be for the United States and China to abjure cyberattacks on each other's critical infrastructure.[30] This proposal was well received by the respondents, with interviewees from across academic, think tank, military, and state organizations all responding positively to this proposal.[31] Respondents appeared to hold relatively similar views of the definition of critical infrastructure to those of their U.S. counterparts—such things as the electrical power grid and the banking system. One respondent noted that there is precedent for such a deal; in early May 2015, just days before we conducted our field interviews, Russia and China announced a general agreement to cooperate with and not attack each other in cyberspace.[32]

The first component of any mutual forbearance proposal is that progress has been made on not attacking critical infrastructure since our interviews in Beijing. In July 2015, the Chinese signed a UN report that called for such attacks to be abjured.[33] There are also indications that the United States and China mutually agree not to attack each other's critical infrastructure—or at least not be the first to do so.[34] As of this writing, however, there is little indication that these agreements have evolved from the trust-us-not-to stage to something that is verifiable. This is why two more components to such an agreement are crucial to fulfill the purposes of the first component.

---

[30] One respondent argued that defining *critical infrastructure* would not be easy because an exact definition might be sensitive. It might take a cyber Red Cross to do so credibly. But, in our view, even an inexact definition would suffice, as long as it was unambiguous.

[31] Author interviews, 2015.

[32] Andrey Ostroukh, "Russia, China Forge Closer Ties with New Economic, Financing Accords," *Wall Street Journal*, May 8, 2015.

[33] UN General Assembly (70th session), "Group of Governmental Experts on Developments in the Field of Information and Telecommunications in the Context of International Security," July 22, 2015.

[34] David E. Sanger, "U.S. and China Seek Arms Deal for Cyberspace," *New York Times*, September 19, 2015.

As a second, and logically entailed, component of any mutual forbearance proposal, the United States and China could also agree not to carry out cyber espionage on each other's critical infrastructure. The rationale for this step is that cyber espionage is almost always a prerequisite for a cyberattack and that it is impossible to distinguish intrusions for the purposes of cyber espionage from an imminent attack if detected by the target. If the two sides have no intent to attack each other's critical infrastructure, they have no need to compromise each other's critical infrastructure systems either, particularly if carried out by inserting malicious code into the target infrastructure. Indeed, both cyber espionage and cyberattack typically entail the prior implantation of computer code in target systems, which then periodically calls back (beacons) to the attacker for further instruction. Implants make subsequent penetrations much easier because the attackers are already inside the target's systems. Banning cyber espionage against critical infrastructure would make it much more difficult to quickly carry out cyberattacks on such infrastructure. Without preplanning and cyber espionage, it could take weeks, months, or even years to carry out such attacks, but if potential adversaries are already inside each other's critical infrastructure, attacks can be carried out almost instantaneously.

Such a ban, if enacted by the two sides, would have several advantages.

First, if successfully executed, a ban would enhance stability, since it would remove critically important systems from being targeted.

Second, a ban would raise the costs of targeting such systems (since, if China were discovered doing so, it would violate the country's given word, potentially affecting its ability to credibly negotiate on other issues in the future), while simultaneously addressing the problem of time that cyberattacks prepared in advance can pose.

Third, such an agreement, if fully realized, would reduce the prospect of accidental conflict by committing the two sides not just to not attacking each other's critical infrastructure but to staying away from it completely, thereby eliminating the possibility of misunderstanding a cyber espionage effort as an imminent attack.

While our respondents generally declined to explicitly agree with this second aspect of our proposal, they did not explicitly push back either. They understood the logic that linked attacks to espionage and that, if one foreswears attacking a system, the rationale for spying on it is that much weaker. Yet, the respondents did not feel quite so comfortable with the notion of foreswearing all espionage against U.S. critical infrastructure.

The third component of a mutual forbearance pact would focus on attribution and an agreement to impose consequences.[35] Yet, in some ways, the problem is not merely or even mostly technical,[36] but political: What arrangements would persuade China to accept evidence (without, at the same time, making it difficult to draw reasonable conclusions from such evidence)?[37] If there were a mutually agreed process for attribution and if China could be counted on to respond appropriately when the process indicates that an attack on the critical infrastructure were traced to China, the threat from China to U.S. critical infrastructure (and vice versa) would be correspondingly reduced. Part of the political problem is that the United States catches China spying far more often than the other way around. China claims that it experiences frequent attacks from the United States (which remains, for instance, the leading source of bots and botnet command-and-control servers), but has forwarded no evidence that the U.S. government

---

[35] It is not necessary that all, most, or even a substantial share of all intrusions be detected and attributed—as might be the case for a deterrence policy. It is necessary, however, that some intrusions be detected with sufficient confidence that there is little doubt that someone cheated.

[36] Few major cyberattacks remain unattributed these days; if the intelligence community is mum, there are private companies that will offer their opinion to those who ask. But the evidence that supports such assertions is less commonly presented (the intelligence community dislikes revealing its methods, and private companies are not much more open). The lack of transparency behind attribution allows the accused to assert innocence and not appear unconvincing in doing so.

[37] Not all attribution evidence is publicly releasable (see David E. Sanger and Martin Fackler, "N.S.A. Breached North Korean Networks Before Sony Attack, Officials Say," *New York Times*, January 18, 2015). This suggests an unbridgeable difference between the confidence that U.S. officials place in attribution and the confidence felt by a fair-minded individual working from open sources but unwilling to take the word of U.S. sources at face value.

protects hackers (or at least private hackers) or carries out specific intrusions.[38]

China's reluctance to accept U.S. accusations of Chinese hacking may reflect the fact that China cannot detect and attribute U.S. cyber espionage as well as the United States can detect and attribute China's cyber espionage. This fact is based on three differences: China's operational security lags U.S. capabilities; China's ability to detect intrusions lags U.S. capabilities; China's ability to attribute detected intrusions lags U.S. capabilities.[39] As long as China's attribution capabilities substantially lag U.S. capabilities, it may be hard to convince China that such a deal would be fair. Worse, until China gains confidence in its own attribution capabilities, it may not believe that U.S. attribution capabilities are particularly good either.[40] Several respondents indicated that it would be difficult to have a meaningful agreement without improvements in China's attribution capabilities.

There are several potential approaches to developing a trustworthy attribution mechanism. However, none of them uncontestably solves the problem, and many would be politically difficult for one or both sides to adopt. One option would be to develop a standing, bilateral fact-finding body to investigate claims of cyberattack. The advantages to this approach would be that both sides, having participated in the deliberations, would be more likely to accept the outcome of any joint investigation. Such an approach would encounter some risk. A concern for the United States would be that China's participation in any such body would be beholden to its government and would there-

---

[38] That the United States puts more resources into investigating crimes against itself than crimes against other countries is more plausible, but also universal and very different from stonewalling.

[39] In the United States, a large share of detection and intrusions are carried out by private companies (many staffed with former NSA employees). China is only starting to develop its own cybersecurity companies (see, for instance, "China Hackers Defect to Other Side, Become Cyber Gatekeepers," *Japan Times*, June 30, 2015). Given this, the United States can buy cybersecurity expertise. Even if some U.S. companies might refuse Chinese business, cybersecurity companies outside the United States (e.g., Israel, Russia) are available.

[40] Those caught spying may believe that they have been fairly caught, but absent their testimony to that effect, China's policymaking community may retain its skepticism.

fore be unlikely to be free to conclude that an attack had indeed been carried out by the Chinese government or PLA. China, for its part, may fear that U.S. capabilities are so superior that such a standing body would turn into a U.S.-dominated forum in which China would be reduced to spectator status. Alternately, if China's cyber espionage is indeed sloppier and more broad gauge than U.S. cyber espionage, the cases that are brought to such a body may overwhelmingly or even exclusively be Chinese in origin, which could be both humiliating and disadvantageous for China.

Shifting such a body from a bilateral to a multilateral forum might assuage some of these concerns (since both U.S. and China representation would be diluted). One respondent proposed the International Atomic Energy Agency as a model, but another said it was inappropriate because far more people touch the Internet than interact with their respective country's nuclear establishment. Additionally, it is unclear whether China would perceive a difference if U.S. experts were replaced by experts (many of whom have ties to the United States) from countries seen by China as friends of the United States.

Might these obstacles be lowered if the United States offered to share its insights into attribution techniques with China in return for China's willingness to credit such techniques as evidence of verification and then move to prosecute those who carried out such intrusions? At first glance, such a proposal appears implausible: Under most circumstances, countries do not share strategic technology or operating concepts with potential adversaries. Yet, there have been exceptions to this general pattern. For example, the United States, in pursuit of nuclear stability, encouraged other countries to adopt permissive action links for their nuclear weapons (a technology that prevents such weapons from being used accidentally or at the instigation of unauthorized users). An added benefit is that stronger Chinese attribution capabilities could reduce the chances of a catalytic conflict if China is attacked by someone masquerading as a U.S. source. As a practical matter, the United States need not share what normally would be classified intelligence sources and methods; it can leverage recent improvements in *private* attribution capabilities (most, but not all, of which are associated with U.S.-based companies) to give China more confidence in its own attribution capabilities.

It is worth clarifying that an offer to help bring Chinese attribution capabilities closer to those available in the United States does not mean that the United States would be teaching China how to detect cyber espionage intrusions, how to improve its defenses, or how to keep its own penetrations from being detected by the United States, to say nothing of it having no relationship to improving the efficiency of PRC cyberintrusion or attack capabilities. Granted, an offer to help bring China's attribution capabilities up to the level of the United States would probably help China mask its attacks. Inasmuch as the United States has yet to use such attribution to curb Chinese cyber espionage (and cyberattacks), it is unclear exactly how great a loss that would be.[41] Even if it becomes harder to attribute attacks to China, it would only make a modest difference because China does not admit complicity in the face of considerable evidence today as is.

Our Chinese respondents reacted favorably to this proposition, even when coupled with the implication that the United States would therefore expect China to give more credence to evidence that a particular intrusion set originated in China. Given the sensitivities associated with how attribution is done in the United States, a deal to get China to sign up to an attribution regime in possible return for the United States showing China how it does attribution would likely require substantial additional research and caveating prior to any possible adoption as policy. For China, an agreement to foreswear attacking critical infrastructure would need to be introduced clearly and officially, probably incrementally, and with clear consequences for cheating. Still, this proposal carries some prospect of raising the costs of cyber espionage to the point that lower-grade, nonstrategic (i.e., economic) actions are reduced or eliminated. It also reduces the risk of misattribution due to malicious third-party actors seeking to route their attacks on one

---

[41] If, as a result of this agreement, China took pains to avoid attribution (in part by leveraging what it has learned about how attribution is done), the cost of China's carrying out cyber espionage would go up and, thus, its volume would go down. The cost goes up because of the additional pains China would have to take to avoid attribution, coupled with the intrusions that they may consequently deem too risky in this new environment.

or another side through U.S. or Chinese servers. And it appears to be one area where it might be possible to gain meaningful buy-in and payoffs from the two sides. For such reasons, it may be worth further exploration.

Although using a neutral third-party attribution capability to enforce the no–cyber espionage aspects of such an agreement is, in our opinion, preferable to improving Chinese attribution capabilities, the latter may be an acceptable price to pay to persuade China that it cannot afford to be caught spying on the U.S. critical infrastructure—whereas today China can blithely ignore all the evidence showing it spies where it should not.

CHAPTER FIVE

Conclusions

The global salience of U.S.-China relations and the potential for quarrels over cyberspace to play an increasingly disruptive role in the relationship make it desirable for the two countries to come to some terms over each other's behavior in cyberspace. In the course of our interviews in China in May 2015, most of our interlocutors did not appear to see any agreement with the United States as plausible, likely, or even particularly necessary. While the United States appeared to see the two countries' relationship in cyberspace as untenable, Chinese interviewees in contrast did not seem to see any urgent need to make changes. As a consequence, the September 2015 U.S.-China cybersecurity agreement may have caught our interlocutors as much by surprise as it appeared to catch most of the community that is watching U.S.-China relations (including the authors). As of mid-February 2016 it remains to be seen whether or not the agreement on cyberspace reached at the Xi-Obama summit has effectively resolved the EMCE issue.[1]

Our first conclusion is that, if the United States is determined to adopt a negotiation-based approach that addresses the entire range of Chinese cyber espionage, success is unlikely to take place any time soon, unless the costs to China of refusing to negotiate over the cyber issue can be increased (beyond simply the threat of a canceled or failed summit meeting). This could potentially be accomplished through linking this issue more directly to the broader health of the overall relationship through representations to China at the highest levels or

---

[1]   See the Postscript of this report for more about the bilaterial U.S.-China cyber agreement in September 2015.

to the use of other levers, such as the threat of economic sanctions or retaliation. However, there is no guarantee that a strategy based solely on imposing costs on China for its conduct, sponsorship, or willingness to condone cyber espionage will have the desired effect of reducing Chinese cyber espionage or creating norms on what targets are out of bounds for cyber espionage. This means that a continued effort to resolve differences and establish norms through dialogue and negotiation is highly desirable, even if such an approach may need to be backed up by the threat of cost imposition.

Worryingly, as of May 2015, our Chinese interlocutors did not tend to see direct, bilateral talks with the United States on cybersecurity as a way to achieve much regarding specific norms or limitations on cyberspace activities. Instead, China's approach to the issue of cybersecurity appears in many respects to be focused first and foremost on attempting to articulate and defend a set of values and proposals for the international governance of cyberspace that would redefine cybersecurity away from issues of concern to the United States, such as EMCE and applying the LOAC to cyberspace. In articulating its positions and submitting proposals on cybersecurity to the UN, China has argued for redefining cybersecurity with an eye toward such issues as cyber sovereignty and moving the management of the Internet out of the hands of the United States and the West and into a more China-friendly setting, such as the UN.

Our team hoped that Chinese respondents and interlocutors would present suggestions for changes in U.S. behavior that might form a basis for a deal on important issues, such as EMCE or cyber espionage against critical infrastructure, but we found that there was little to no corresponding set of asks on the Chinese side. This may stem from the relative lack of expertise on a technically complex policy issue, combined with the understandable reluctance of respondents to speak ahead of official policy on a sensitive issue. The few suggestions we heard were either not as pressing to our interlocutors as U.S. concerns are to U.S. officials or would be unacceptable because they would require U.S. officials to make promises that contravened the U.S. Constitution (notably, the First Amendment). Thus, our second conclusion is that any deal with China to restrain EMCE in exchange for something that the United States might be able and willing to offer in the cyber domain is unlikely to be particularly wide ranging or robust unless it is linked to broader cooperation and conflict avoidance in the overall relationship.

We next explored the possibility of achieving progress in cyber-security negotiations by means of an agreement that would have both the United States and China refrain from attacking each other. Here, we found more common ground; our respondents, and Chinese writings more broadly, generally reflect a willingness to agree to such a proposition (although some of our respondents preferred a multilateral approach over a bilateral agreement). Such an agreement would potentially represent a valuable step forward in terms of mutual reassurance and could help consolidate norms that would affirm, clarify, or at least supplement the applicability of the international LOAC to cyberspace. Since China announced an agreement with Russia in May 2015 to refrain from carrying out cyberattacks on each other, there may be precedent to draw on in negotiations with China over such an issue.[2]

A logical codicil of any such agreement on avoiding targeting critical infrastructure was that an agreement not to attack also implied an agreement not to spy on such targets. If one is not planning to attack critical infrastructure, there is no reason for a foreign government to be collecting detailed information on a system's construct and, hence, its vulnerabilities. Additionally, since it is difficult or even impossible to distinguish between evidence of spying on such systems and evidence of intrusions that are preparations for an attack, spying should be abjured by all sides. Here, too, we found some grounds for agreement, although less clear commitment, perhaps because the Chinese we spoke with declined to affirm that victims of cyber espionage could always plausibly and rightfully infer that intrusions constitute preparations for attack.

The last proposition we put to our Chinese interlocutors—that the United States might consider sharing insights into attribution if China agreed to common evidentiary standards and credibly committed to prosecuting those found to have violated these—was the tricki-

---

[2] Cory Bennett, "Russia, China Unite with Major Cyber Pact," *The Hill*, May 8, 2015.

est. Such an agreement would require some mutually approved method of determining when one or the other side had violated its part of the bargain in ways that would have the guilty party admit that it erred. As argued above, the current relative weakness of Chinese attribution capabilities, combined with the high levels of mutual strategic mistrust, suggests that having each side accept the other's prima facie evidence would not work. This suggests that what may be needed for progress is the construction of a bilateral, multilateral, or international cyber-dispute resolution mechanism, supplemented perhaps by U.S. efforts to help China improve its own attribution capabilities.

Such an agreement will not come easily; it carries with it political and potential policy risks and may also not gain China's buy-in. In an environment as troubled by issues of mutual mistrust as the current U.S.-China relationship is, it would be challenging to muster enough U.S. political support for such a step. For their part, many of China's actors are likely to be suspicious of *any* U.S. efforts to shape Chinese views of or capabilities in the cyber domain. Yet, such an approach may be an idea that is worth exploring further in Track Two dialogues and conducting further research on to more completely assess all of its practical, technological, and political implications, and to further flesh out where the main sources of opposition are likely to stem from and how they might be reduced.

Were such a three-part agreement—including a norm of not targeting or intruding into each side's critical infrastructure—combined with an offer to help China improve its attribution capabilities in exchange for a deal to actually follow through on, investigate, and maybe even prosecute cyber intrusions originating in China (or the United States) come into existence, it might change the nature of the two sides' relations in cyberspace across an important swath of issues. To be sure, the two countries would still disagree strongly over such issues as freedom of access to information (United States) versus information control and cyber sovereignty (PRC), efficiency and effectiveness of the current international backbone architecture of the Internet (United States) versus cyber hegemony (PRC), whether both would still engage in cyber-enabled national security espionage, and differences over a host of other issues in cyberspace and beyond. But such a deal, if it could be credibly committed to and followed through on in practice, would represent a substantial improvement of the U.S.-China relationship in cyberspace, for which reason we argue it is worth consideration and additional research.

In conclusion, Chinese and U.S. views of cybersecurity overlap only on a few points, and even where they do, the two sides will find it difficult to make progress on such issues as avoiding targeting of critical infrastructure if the two sides struggle to maintain the progress hinted at in the September 2015 summit agreement on cyberspace. With respect to reaching a broad, meaningful, and lasting agreement on norms about legitimate targets in cyberspace, much work remains to be done, and it is unclear that such a result will indeed be possible. Perhaps the most promising area where we might see some prospect of negotiating a set of norms in the years ahead lies in avoiding targeting or carrying out espionage on critical infrastructure. This could be supported by efforts to create common standards of evidence, define how attribution is to be done, and prosecute those who commit such actions.

Yet any meaningful agreements over cyberspace will not be easy to negotiate. The trends in the bilateral U.S.-China relationship, as well as inside Chinese society more broadly, are not positive at present. While China's willingness to negotiate over these issues could conceivably change substantially in the future if the country were to develop a stronger domestic constituency favoring the protection of intellectual property rights and a more independent and professional legal system, it is hard to see signs of such a development at present. Indeed, given the current realities of China, where all court judges are appointed by the CPC, new lawyers are asked to swear allegiance to the CPC,[3] and rights-defense lawyers [weiquan lushi] are arrested en masse,[4] the prospects of any such broad-ranging, meaningful, and lasting agreement

---

[3] Sui-Lee Wee, "China Orders Lawyers to Swear Allegiance to the Communist Party," Reuters, March 21, 2012.

[4] Chris Buckley, "Chinese Authorities Detain and Denounce Rights Lawyers," New York Times, July 11, 2015; Nash Jenkins, "China Arrested More than 100 Human-Rights Lawyers and Activists over the Weekend," Time, July 12, 2015.

appear slim in the near to middle term. Should China and the United States decide that they both want to negotiate norms over behavior in cyberspace in the future, the research findings presented above might provide some insights in how to do so.

Postscript

On September 25, 2015, as this report was in the process of final production and publication, President Xi came to the United States on an official state visit. During his trip, he and President Obama announced that,

> The United States and China agree that neither country's government will conduct or knowingly support cyber-enabled theft of intellectual property, including trade secrets or other confidential business information, with the intent of providing competitive advantages to companies or commercial sectors.

They also agreed to

> cooperate . . . with requests to investigate cybercrimes . . . [make a] common effort to further identify and promote appropriate norms of state behavior in cyberspace . . . [and] establish a high-level joint dialogue mechanism on fighting cybercrime and related issues.[1]

Thus, after a relatively brief period of negotiations just before the summit, the Chinese president committed his country to recognize and adhere to norms of cyber espionage that disallowed most of the Chinese behavior that the United States objects to while placing no new restrictions on the kinds of cyber behavior the U.S. regards

---

[1] White House, "Fact Sheet: President Xi Jinping's State Visit to the United States," Washington, D.C., September 25, 2015.

as legitimate.[2] This agreement was, to say the least, a distinct departure from past U.S.-China interactions over the cyber issue. Moreover, while, in retrospect, we could have found indications that such an outcome was not beyond the scope of possibility (e.g., because none of our interlocutors defended EMCE), it was hardly a predictable outcome, either, and not something that, to the best of our knowledge, any serious commentators on either side of the Pacific had predicted before the summit took place.

What does this agreement mean, and why did China make it? Despite the likelihood that clarifying facts will emerge after this is written and that the story of U.S.-China interactions will continue to develop, we nevertheless offer several possible explanations. These are not mutually exclusive, and all may have played a role; they are phrased as prospective future outcomes and explanations since they have yet to play out:

- *The agreement will not lead to major change.* China might well continue carrying out EMCE.[3] Even if the United States can detect and attribute the intrusions, China's government could continue to deny its complicity (or will argue that "China is a big country, and we can't know everything that you say goes on here"). No monitoring system has been established that both sides agreed to accept the results of (nor was there talk to how to set one up). The Chinese government did not lose face with this agreement because it has never officially argued that EMCE is no worse than national security cyber espionage, nor has it ever admitted to engaging in EMCE (thereby implying that the agreement will not change anything because there was China-sourced EMCE going on previously). Indeed, President Xi denounced EMCE while he was still in Seattle, before the agreement was announced.

---

[2] Note, for instance, that commercial espionage—which the United States, until 2013, said it did not do—is allowed, as long as the results are not given to commercial firms.

[3] Early evidence of continued penetration attempts after the summit ended suggests that China's EMCE did not come to an immediate cold stop; see Paul Mozur, "Cybersecurity Firm Says Chinese Hackers Keep Attacking U.S. Companies," *New York Times*, October 20, 2015.

- *This agreement will lead to measurable change, and it came about under pressure.* Two types of pressure may have been involved. The first type of pressure was the threat of U.S. sanctions, which perhaps caused China to fold. Despite having an economy about two-thirds the size of that of the United States, perhaps China felt that it would be in a vulnerable position due to recent unfavorable economic trends. Its economy is shaky (the Shanghai stock market index deflated substantially in summer 2015 despite public attempts to keep the air in); it lacks the many allies enjoyed by the United States who might assist its efforts in a confrontation; its military is still substantially inferior; it fears U.S. hegemony in cyberspace; and it lacks the soft power of the United States. Because China's economy depends more on exports to the United States than vice versa, it could lose more in an all-out trade war. Lastly, the United States appeared ready to run escalatory risks on Chinese cyber espionage, when what started as injury became insult with the OPM hack. If China's willingness to reach an agreement on norms of targeting in cyberspace reflects its assessment of the correlation of forces, so to speak, this agreement may be meaningful and long standing. The second type of pressure may have arisen because China's leadership came to the conclusion that China's activities in cyberspace were creating unacceptably high levels of risk for the U.S.-China relationship and sought to dial down tensions in this arena to avoid the prospect of all-out U.S.-China strategic competition and confrontation.[4]
- *China was ready to concede because the value of EMCE to them is disappointing (or declining).* Perhaps China is simply not getting very much from stealing intellectual property anymore (i.e., it takes more than stealing a good cookbook to be a world-renowned chef). By way of example, the bill of particulars associated with the indictment of the five PLA officers shows very little

---

[4] This comment reflects a logic that the preceding paragraph seeks to build on, that the fact that China's leaders value stability in the overall relationship with the United States. If cyber is seen as imperiling this, the leadership may change its view of the value of unfettered cyber if that is imposing costs that are risking broader geostrategic instability.

intellectual property theft in comparison with the taking of business proprietary data.[5] In any negotiation, it pays to trade away something that the other side values more than you do as a way of getting them to concede things that really matter to you. Thus, China conceded on this issue so that it could stand firm on other issues.[6] That noted, there is no evidence since the summit that the United States itself made any quid-pro-quo concessions.

- Lastly, China wanted to rein in its own freelance hackers, and this deal gives Beijing more authority to do just that (just as the December 2014 climate deal gave Beijing more authority to put the squeeze on provincial and country governments to get serious about pollution). China's leadership may fear that unconstrained freelance or moonlighting hackers threaten good order in the country in general. They may fear such hackers turning their sights from foreign firms to Chinese firms, perhaps discouraging the latter from investing in their own product development. Worse, from Beijing's perspective, they may turn their hacking skills against the central government. Chinese officials may also leverage this agreement to further professionalize its own hacking community. They may have been embarrassed to be likened to drunken burglars by the Federal Bureau of Investigation's director and were surely sorely embarrassed by a lead story in the *Wall Street Journal* that exposed a Chinese military link to hacking, published two days before the President Xi's arrival at the White House.[7]

Chinese leaders appear to believe (if postsummit discussions with a small number of Chinese interlocutors are indicative) that the agree-

---

[5] Department of Justice, Office of Public Affairs, "U.S. Charges Five Chinese Military Hackers for Cyber Espionage Against U.S. Corporations and a Labor Organization for Commercial Advantage," Washington, D.C., May 19, 2014.

[6] Jack Goldsmith (former Assistant Attorney General) mulled whether the United States may have agreed to stop undermining China's Great Firewall. See Jack Goldsmith, "What Explains the U.S.-China Cyber 'Agreement?'" *Lawfare blog*, September 26, 2015.

[7] Josh Chin, "Cyber Sleuths Track Hacker to China's Military," *Wall Street Journal*, September 23, 2015.

ment gives China breathing space from U.S. threats of economic sanctions. They could well argue that the United States cannot argue that the Chinese have not kept their word until it finds an objectionable act of EMCE that *started after the agreement* was made. Thus, continued talk of sanctions or other forms of pressure are in bad faith. But it is unclear whether such expectations will be met. Subsequent weeks have featured news stories about which specific Chinese companies would be targeted with sanctions and reports that the Chinese, under U.S. pressure, have arrested their own citizens over EMCE accusations.[8] As of February 2016, the final meaning of and explanation for the U.S.-China agreement on relations in cyberspace had yet to play out.[9]

---

[8] Hannah Kuchler, Geoff Dyer, Gina Chon, Lucy Hornby, and Demetri Savastopulo, "U.S. Targets Chinese Groups in Cyber Feud," *Financial Times*, October 7, 2015, p. 1; Ellen Nakashima and Adam Goldman, "In a First, Chinese Hackers Are Arrested at the Behest of the U.S. Government," *Washington Post*, October 9, 2015. As of October 12, 2015, this reportage had yet to be confirmed by similar reportage in the *New York Times*.

[9] Reports emerged in fall 2015 in which some observers see the Chinese military as having reduced its involvement in EMCE, with the Chinese Ministry of State Security possibly having taken over this role to a greater extent than was previously the case, with other observers seeing a continued high level of intellectual property theft stemming from the actions of nonstate actors in China. See, for example, Shannon Tiezzi, "U.S., China Open New High-Level Cyber Talks," *The Diplomat*, December 2, 2015.

References

"Admit Nothing and Deny Everything," *The Economist*, June 8, 2013. As of December 2, 2015:
http://www.economist.com/news/china/21579044-barack-obama-says-he-ready -talk-xi-jinping-about-chinese-cyber-attacks-makes-one

Alperovich, Dmitri, *Revealed: Operation Shady RAT*, white paper, Santa Clara, Calif.: McAfee, August 3, 2011. As of December 2, 2015:
http://www.mcafee.com/us/resources/white-papers/wp-operation-shady-rat.pdf

"An International Code of Conduct for Information Security—China's Perspective on Building a Peaceful, Secure, Open and Cooperative Cyberspace," statement prepared for a conference in Geneva hosted by the UN Institute for Disarmament Research, February 10, 2014. As of November 30, 2015:
http://www.unidir.ch/files/conferences/pdfs/a-cyber-code-of-conduct-the-best -vehicle-for-progress-en-1-963.pdf

Austin, Greg, "No Easy Solutions in US-China Cyber Security," *East Asia Forum*, October 6, 2015. As of December 1, 2015:
http://www.eastasiaforum.org/2015/10/06 /no-easy-solutions-in-us-china-cyber-security

Axelrod, Robert, *The Evolution of Cooperation*, New York: BasicBooks, 1984.

Bhattacharjee, Yudhijit, "A New Kind of Spy: How China Obtains American Technological Secrets," *New Yorker*, May 5, 2014. As of December 2, 2015:
http://www.newyorker.com/magazine/2014/05/05/a-new-kind-of-spy

Beech, Eric, and Ben Blanchard, "U.S., Chinese Officials Meet on Cyber Security Issues: White House," Reuters, September 12, 2015. As of December 1, 2015:
http://www.reuters.com/article/2015/09/13 /us-usa-china-cybersecurity-idUSKCN0RC0S420150913

Bennett, Cory, "Russia, China Unite with Major Cyber Pact," *The Hill*, May 8, 2015. As of December 2, 2015:
http://thehill.com/policy /cybersecurity/241453-russia-china-unit-with-major-cyber-pact

Blackwill, Robert D., and Ashley J. Tellis, *Revising U.S. Grand Strategy Toward China*, Washington, D.C.: Council on Foreign Relations, Council Special Report No. 72, May 2015. As of November 30, 2015:
http://carnegieendowment.org/files/Tellis_Blackwill.pdf

Bodeen, Christopher, "U.S. Says Hacking Undermines China's Interests," *Pioneer Press*, April 9, 2013. As of December 2, 2015:
http://www.twincities.com/ci_22984979
/us-says-hacking-undermines-chinas-interests

Braun, Stephen, "Official Says Hackers Hit Up to 25,000 Homeland Security Employees," *Washington Post*, August 23, 2014. As of November 30, 2015:
https://www.washingtonpost.com/business/economy/official-says-hackers-hit-up
-to-25000-homeland-security-employees/2014/08/22/a855b6c0-2a52-11e4-958c-
268a320a60ce_story.html

Buckley, Chris, "China Takes Aim at Western Ideas," *New York Times*, August 19, 2013. As of December 1, 2015:
http://www.nytimes.com/2013/08/20/world/asia/chinas-new-leadership-takes
-hard-line-in-secret-memo.html

———, "Chinese Authorities Detain and Denounce Rights Lawyers," *New York Times*, July 11, 2015. As of December 2, 2015:
http://www.nytimes.com/2015/07/12/world/asia/china-arrests-human-rights
-lawyers-zhou-shifeng.html

"Canada National Research Council 'Hacked by Chinese Spies,'" BBC, July 29, 2014.

Carr, Jeffrey, "Cyber Attacks: Why Retaliating Against China Is the Wrong Reaction," *The Diplomat*, August 6, 2015. As of December 1, 2015:
http://thediplomat.com/2015/08
/cyber-attacks-why-retaliating-against-china-is-the-wrong-reaction

Center for Strategic and International Studies, *The Economic Impact of Cybercrime and Cyber Espionage*, July 2013. As of November 30, 2015:
http://www.mcafee.com/us/resources/reports/rp-economic-impact-cybercrime.pdf

———, "Significant Cyber Incidents since 2006," March 10, 2014. As of December 2, 2015:
http://csis.org/files/publication/140310_Significant_Cyber_Incidents_Since
_2006.pdf

Chang, Amy, *Warring State: China's Cybersecurity Strategy*, Washington, D.C.: Center for a New American Security, December 2015, pp. 7, 10. As of November 30, 2015:
http://www.cnas.org/sites/default/files/publications-pdf/CNAS_WarringState
_Chang_report_010615.pdf

Chen, Te-Ping, "Snowden Alleges U.S. Hacking in China," *Wall Street Journal*, June 23, 2013. As of December 2, 2015:
http://www.wsj.com/articles/SB10001424127887324577904578562483284884530

Chen Weihua and Li Xiaokun, "China Demands Charges Be Dropped," *China Daily*, May 22, 2014. As of November 30, 2015:
http://usa.chinadaily.com.cn/epaper/2014-05/22/content_17533404.htm

Cheng, Dean, "Chinese Views on Deterrence," *Joint Forces Quarterly*, No. 60, spring 2011, pp. 92–94.

Chin, Josh, "Cyber Sleuths Track Hacker to China's Military," *Wall Street Journal*, September 23, 2015. As of December 2, 2015:
http://www.wsj.com/articles/
cyber-sleuths-track-hacker-to-chinas-military-1443042030

"China Behind Cyberattack on US Sites, Report Says," *San Francisco Chronicle*, May 8, 2015. As of December 1, 2015:
http://www.sfgate.com/news/article/China-behind-cyberattack-on-U-S-sites
-report-6252140.php

"China Hackers Defect to Other Side, Become Cyber Gatekeepers," *Japan Times*, June 30, 2015. As of December 2, 2015:
http://www.japantimes.co.jp/news/2015/06/30/asia-pacific/china-hackers-defect
-side-become-cyber-gatekeepers/#.Vl-dm2SDFBc

"China's Head of Cyberspace Discusses How to Build Mutual Trust with U.S.," *GW Today*, December 3, 2014. As of December 1, 2015:
http://gwtoday.gwu.edu
/china%E2%80%99s-head-cyberspace-discusses-how-build-mutual-trust-us

"China Voice: Drop Cold War Mentality on China's Cybersecurity," Xinhua, April 22, 2014. As of December 2, 2015:
http://english.cntv.cn/2014/04/22/ARTI1398148113852301.shtml

Cho, Meeyoung, "Low-Risk 'Worm' Removed at Hacked South Korea Nuclear Operator," Reuters, December 30, 2014. As of December 1, 2015:
http://www.reuters.com/article/2014/12/30
/nuclear-southkorea-cybersecurity-idUSL3N0UE1A320141230

Chung, Jae Ho, "China's Evolving Views of the Korean-American Alliance, 1953–2012," *Journal of Contemporary China*, Vol. 23, No. 87, 2014, pp. 425–442.

Claburn, Thomas, "Chinese Hackers Angered by Microsoft's Epic Fail," *Information Week*, October 23, 2008. As of December 2, 2015:
http://www.informationweek.com/software/operating-systems
/chinese-hackers-angered-by-microsofts-epic-fail/d/d-id/1073270?

Clapper, James R., "Statement of Record: Worldwide Threat Assessment of the U.S. Intelligence Community," Washington, D.C.: Director of National Intelligence, February 26, 2015. As of December 2, 2015:
http://www.dni.gov/files/documents/Unclassified_2015_ATA_SFR_-_SASC_FINAL.pdf

Clayton, Mark, "Exclusive: Cyberattack Leaves Natural Gas Pipelines Vulnerable to Sabotage," *Christian Science Monitor*, February 27, 2013. As of December 2, 2015:
http://www.csmonitor.com/Environment/2013/0227/Exclusive-Cyberattack-leaves-natural-gas-pipelines-vulnerable-to-sabotage

CSIS—*See* Center for Strategic and International Studies.

Culpan, Tim, "Decade-Long Cyberspy Attack Hacked Southeast Asian Targets," Bloomberg, April 12, 2015. As of December 2, 2015:
http://www.bloomberg.com/news/articles/2015-04-12/decade-long-cyber-spying-campaign-hacked-southeast-asia-targets

Deeks, Ashley, "Tallinn 2.0 and a Chinese View of the Tallinn Process," *Lawfare blog*, May 31, 2015. As of November 30, 2015:
https://www.lawfareblog.com/tallinn-20-and-chinese-view-tallinn-process

Dilanian, Ken, "NSA Director: China Can Damage U.S. Power Grid," Associated Press, November 20, 2014. As of November 30, 2015:
http://www.salon.com/2014/11/20/nsa_director_china_can_damage_us_power_grid

Dong Qingling, "Confidence-Building for Cybersecurity Between China and the United States," *China International Studies*, July/August 2014, pp. 57–68. As of November 30, 2015:
http://www.ciis.org.cn/english/2014-09/23/content_7254470.htm

"The Dragon's New Teeth," *The Economist*, April 7, 2012. As of December 1, 2015:
http://www.economist.com/node/21552193

"Espionage Report: Merkel's China Visit Marred by Hacking Allegations," *Spiegel* online, August 27, 2007. As of December 2, 2015:
http://www.spiegel.de/international/world/espionage-report-merkel-s-china-visit-marred-by-hacking-allegations-a-502169.html

Fletcher, Owen, "China Game Boss Sniped Rivals, Took Down Internet," *PC World*, August 29, 2009. As of December 2, 2015:
http://www.pcworld.com/article/171018/article.html

Fisher, Roger, William Ury, and Bruce Patton, *Getting to Yes: Negotiating Agreement Without Giving In*, London: Penguin Publishing, 1981.

Frizell, Sam, "NSA Director on Sony Hack: 'The Entire World Is Watching,'" *Time*, January 8, 2015. As of December 1, 2015:
http://time.com/3660757/nsa-michael-rogers-sony-hack

Gantz, John F., Joe Howard, Richard Lee, Harish N. Taori, Ricardo Villate, Christian A. Christiansen, Albert Wang, Christian Lachawitz, Thomas Vavra, Rich Rodolfo, Attaphon Satidkanitkul, Ravikant Sharma, Alejandro Florean, Stephen Minton, and Marcel Warmerdam, *The Dangerous World of Counterfeit and Pirated Software: How Pirated Software Can Compromise the Cybersecurity of Consumers, Enterprises, and Nations . . . and the Resultant Costs in Time and Money*, Framingham, Mass.: International Data Corporation, 2013. As of December 2, 2015:
http://news.microsoft.com/download/presskits/antipiracy/docs/IDC030513.pdf

Gaouette, Nicole, and Brendan Greeley, "U.S. Funds Help Democracy Activists Evade Internet Crackdowns," Bloomberg, April 20, 2011. As of December 2, 2015:
http://www.bloomberg.com/news/articles/2011-04-20/u-s-funds-help-democracy-activists-evade-internet-crackdowns

Garamone, Jim, "Cybercom Chief Details Cyberspace Defense," American Forces Press Service, September 23, 2010. As of February 12, 2016:
http://archive.defense.gov/news/newsarticle.aspx?id=60987

"German Government and Companies Attacked by Chinese Hackers," *Want China Times*, February 26, 2013.

Godwin, Paul H. B., and Alice L. Miller, *China's Forbearance Has Limits: Chinese Threat and Retaliation Signaling and Its Implications for a Sino-American Military Confrontation*, Washington, D.C.: National Defense University Press, April 2013. As of December 2, 2015:
http://ndupress.ndu.edu/Portals/68/Documents/stratperspective/china/ChinaPerspectives-6.pdf

Goldsmith, Jack, "What Explains the U.S.-China Cyber 'Agreement?'" *Lawfare blog*, September 26, 2015. As of December 2, 2015:
https://www.lawfareblog.com/what-explains-us-china-cyber-agreement

Goldstein, Lyle J., "How China Sees America's Moves in Asia: Worse than Containment," *National Interest*, October 29, 2014. As of November 30, 2015:
http://nationalinterest.org/feature/how-china-sees-americas-moves-asia-worse-containment-11560

———, *Meeting China Halfway*, Washington, D.C.: Georgetown University Press, 2015.

Gorman, Siobhan, and Julian E. Barnes, "Cyber Combat: Act of War," *Wall Street Journal*, May 31, 2011. As of December 2, 2015:
http://www.wsj.com/articles/SB10001424052702304563104576355623135782718

Gorman, Siobhan, August Cole, and Yochi Dreazen, "Computer Spies Breach Fighter-Jet Project," *Wall Street Journal*, April 21, 2009. As of December 2, 2015: http://www.wsj.com/articles/SB124027491029837401

Grigsby, Alex, "The UN GGE on Cybersecurity: What is the UN's Role?" Council on Foreign Relations *(Net Politics blog)*, April 15, 2015. As of December 2, 2015: http://blogs.cfr.org/cyber/2015/04/15/ the-un-gge-on-cybersecurity-what-is-the-uns-role/

Gullo, Karen, "California Man Guilty of Stealing DuPont Trade Secrets," *Bloomberg Business*, March 5, 2014. As of December 2, 2015: http://www.bloomberg.com/news/articles/2014-03-05 /california-man-guilty-of-stealing-dupont-trade-secrets

Guo Ji, "Cyber Should Not Become a New Tool of American Hegemony: Starting from an Explanation of the 'PRISM-gate' Incident [Wangluo buying chengwei Meiguo baquan xi gongju: Cong 'Lingjingmen' shijian shuokai qu]," *Seeking Truth* [*Qiu Shi*], No. 15, 2013, pp. 57–59.

Ikenberry, G. John, *After Victory: Institutions, Strategic Restraint, and the Rebuilding of Order After Major Wars*, Princeton, N.J.: Princeton University Press, 2000.

Inkster, Nigel, "Chinese Intelligence in the Cyber Age," *Survival*, Vol. 55, No. 1, February–March 2013, pp. 45–66.

Jackson, David, "Obama, China's Xi to Hold Tense Meetings on Cybersecurity, Military," *USA Today*, September 21, 2015. As of December 1, 2015: http://www.usatoday.com/story/news/2015/09/21 /obama-china-xi-jinping-white-house-meeting-cybersecurity/72519380

Jenkins, Nash "China Arrested More than 100 Human-Rights Lawyers and Activists over the Weekend," *Time*, July 12, 2015. As of December 2, 2015: http://time.com/3954935/china-arrests-lawyers-human-rights

Jiang Chong, "Cyber: The Invisible New Battlefront [*Wangluo: Kanbujian de xin zhanxian*]," *Seeking Truth* [*Qiu Shi*], No. 13, 2010, pp. 53–55.

Jiang Li, Zhang Xiaolan, and Xu Feibiao, "The International Cybersecurity Dilemma and a Way Out [uoji wangluo anquan hezuo de kunjing yu chulu]," *Contemporary International Relations* [*Xiandai guoji guanxi*], No. 9, 2013, pp. 52–58.

Kang, Cecilia, "Hillary Clinton Calls for Web Freedom, Demands China Investigate Google Attack," *Washington Post*, January 22, 2010. As of February 12, 2016: http://www.washingtonpost.com/wp-dyn/content/article/2010/01/21 /AR2010012101699.html

Kravets, David, "FBI Director Says Chinese Hackers Are Like a 'Drunk Burglar,'" *Ars Technica*, October 6, 2014. As of December 2, 2015:
http://arstechnica.com/tech-policy/2014/10
/fbi-director-says-chinese-hackers-are-like-a-drunk-burglar

Krebs, Brian, "Chinese Hackers Blamed for Intrusion at Energy Industry Giant Telvent," *Krebs on Security*, September 12, 2012. As of December 2, 2015:
http://krebsonsecurity.com/2012/09
/chinese-hackers-blamed-for-intrusion-at-energy-industry-giant-telvent/

Krekel, Brian, George Bakos, and Christopher Barnett, *Capability of the People's Republic of China to Conduct Cyber Warfare and Computer Network Exploitation*, Washington, D.C.: The U.S.-China Economic and Security Review Commission, 2009. As of December 2, 2015:
http://nsarchive.gwu.edu/NSAEBB/NSAEBB424/docs/Cyber-030.pdf

Kuchler, Hannah, Geoff Dyer, Gina Chon, Lucy Hornby, and Demetri Savastopulo, "U.S. Targets Chinese Groups in Cyber Feud," *Financial Times*, October 7, 2015, p. 1. As of December 2, 2015:
http://www.ft.com/intl/cms/s/0/4ba9e99a-6d0f-11e5-aca9-d87542bf8673.html

Lagorio, Christine, "State Department Computers Hacked," CBS News, July 11, 2006. As of December 2, 2015:
http://www.cbsnews.com/news/state-department-computers-hacked

Lam, Lana, "NSA Targeted China's Tsinghua University in Extensive Hacking Attacks, Says Snowden," *South China Morning Post*,
June 22, 2013. As of December 2, 2015:
http://www.scmp.com/news/china/article/1266892
/exclusive-nsa-targeted-chinas-tsinghua-university-extensive-hacking?page=all

Lampton, David M. "A Tipping Point in US-China Relations Is Upon Us," *US-China Perception Monitor*, May 11, 2015. As of November 30, 2015:
http://www.uscnpm.org/blog/2015/05/11/a-tipping-point-in-u-s-china-relations
-is-upon-us-part-i

Landler, Mark, and David E. Sanger, "U.S. Demands China Block Cyberattacks and Agree to Rules," *New York Times*, March 12, 2013. As of December 2, 2015:
http://www.nytimes.com/2013/03/12/world/asia/us-demands-that-china-end-
hacking-and-set-cyber-rules.html

Lieberthal, Kenneth, and Wang Jisi, *Addressing U.S.-China Strategic Distrust*, Washington, D.C.: The John L. Thornton China Center, Brookings Institution, 2012. As of November 30, 2015:
http://www.brookings.edu/~/media/research/files/papers/2012/3/30-us-china
-lieberthal/0330_china_lieberthal.pdf

Lieberthal, Kenneth, and Peter W. Singer, *Cybersecurity and U.S.-China Relations*, Washington, D.C.: 21st Century Defense Initiative, The John L. Thornton China Center, Brookings Institution, February 2012. As of November 30, 2015: http://www.brookings.edu/~/media/Research/Files/Papers/2012/2/23 %20cybersecurity%20china%20us%20singer%20liberthal/0223_cybersecurit y_china_us_lieberthal_singer_pdf_english.PDF

Lindsay, Jon R., Tai Ming Cheung, and Derek Reveron, *China and Cybersecurity: Espionage , Strategy, and Politics in the Digital Domain*, Oxford: Oxford University Press, 2015.

"Look Who's Listening," *Economist*, June 15, 2013. As of December 2, 2015: http://www.economist.com/news/briefing/21579473-americas-national-security -agency-collects-more-information-most-people-thought-will

Lu Chuanying, "An Attempt to Analyze the Current Global Governance Dilemma in Cyberspace [Shixi dangqian wangluo kongjian quanqiu zhili kunjing]," *Contemporary International Relations* [*Xiandai guoji guanxi*], No. 11, 2013, pp. 48–54.

Ma Xinming, "What Kind of Internet Order Do We Need?" *Chinese Journal of International Law*, Vol. 14, No. 2, 2015, pp. 399–403. As of November 30, 2015: http://chinesejil.oxfordjournals.org/content/14/2/399.short

Mandiant, *APT1: Exposing One of China's Cyber Espionage Units*, March 2013. As of December 1, 2015: http://intelreport.mandiant.com/Mandiant_APT1_Report.pdf

Markoff, John, and David Barboza, "Researchers Trace Data Theft to Intruders in China,"*New York Times*, April 5, 2010. As of December 2, 2015: http://www.nytimes.com/2010/04/06/science/06cyber.html

Mastro, Oriana Skylar, "Why Chinese Assertiveness Is Here to Stay," *Washington Quarterly*, Vol. 37, No. 4, winter 2015, pp. 151–170.

McAfee Foundstone Professional Services and McAfee Labs, *Global Energy Cyberattacks: "Night Dragon,"* white paper, Santa Clara, Calif.: McAfee, February 10, 2011. As of December 2, 2015: http://www.mcafee.com/us/resources/white-papers/wp-global-energy -cyberattacks-night-dragon.pdf

McReynolds, Joe, "Chinese Thinking on Cyber Deterrence," in Philip C. Saunders and Andrew Scobell, eds., *PLA Influence on Chinese National Security Policymaking*, Stanford, Calif.: Stanford University Press, 2015.

Miller, Joe, "Israeli Iron Dome Firms 'Infiltrated by Chinese Hackers,'" BBC, July 31, 2014. As of December 2, 2015: http://www.bbc.com/news/technology-28583283

Mozur, Paul, "Cybersecurity Firm Says Chinese Hackers Keep Attacking U.S. Companies," *New York Times*, October 20, 2015. As of December 21, 2015:
http://www.nytimes.com/2015/10/20/technology/cybersecurity-firm-says-chinese-hackers-keep-attacking-us-companies.html

———, "New Rules in China Upset Western Tech Companies," *New York Times*, January 29, 2015. As of November 30, 2015:
http://www.nytimes.com/2015/01/29/technology/in-china-new-cybersecurity-rules-perturb-western-tech-companies.html

Nakashima, Ellen, "Indictment of PLA Hackers Is Part of Broad U.S. Strategy to Curb Chinese Cyberspying," *Washington Post*, May 22, 2014. As of December 1, 2015:
https://www.washingtonpost.com/world/national-security/indictment-of-pla-hackers-is-part-of-broad-us-strategy-to-curb-chinese-cyberspying/2014/05/22/a66cf26a-e1b4-11e3-9743-bb9b59cde7b9_story.html

———, "Security Firm Finds Link Between China and Anthem Hack," *Washington Post*, February 27, 2015a. As of November 30, 2015:
https://www.washingtonpost.com/news/the-switch/wp/2015/02/27/security-firm-finds-link-between-china-and-anthem-hack

———, "With Series of Major Hacks, China Builds Database on Americans," *Washington Post*, June 5, 2015b. As of November 30, 2015:
https://www.washingtonpost.com/world/national-security/in-a-series-of-hacks-china-appears-to-building-a-database-on-americans/2015/06/05/d2af51fa-0ba3-11e5-95fd-d580f1c5d44e_story.html

———, "U.S. Developing Sanctions Against China over Economic Spying," *Washington Post*, August 30, 2015c. As of December 1, 2015:
https://www.washingtonpost.com/world/national-security/administration-developing-sanctions-against-china-over-cyberespionage/2015/08/30/9b2910aa-480b-11e5-8ab4-c73967a143d3_story.html

Nakashima, Ellen, and Adam Goldman, "In a First, Chinese Hackers Are Arrested at the Behest of the U.S. Government," *Washington Post*, October 9, 2015. As of December 2, 2015:
https://www.washingtonpost.com/world/national-security/in-a-first-chinese-hackers-are-arrested-at-the-behest-of-the-us-government/2015/10/09/0a7b0e46-6778-11e5-8325-a42b5a459b1e_story.html

Nathan, Andrew J., and Andrew Scobell, "How China Sees America: The Sum of Beijing's Fears," *Foreign Affairs*, September/October 2012. As of November 30, 2015:
https://www.foreignaffairs.com/articles/china/2012-08-16/how-china-sees-america

Novetta, "Cyber Security Coalition Releases Full Report on Large-Scale Interdiction of Chinese State Sponsored Espionage Effort," Washington, D.C., October 28, 2014. As of December 2, 2015:
https://www.novetta.com/2014/10/cyber-security-coalition-releases-full-report-on -large-scale-interdiction-of-chinese-state-sponsored-espionage-effort

Obama, Barack, "Executive Order—'Blocking the Property of Certain Persons Engaging in Significant Malicious Cyber-Enabled Activities,'" Washington, D.C.: The White House, April 1, 2015. As of December 2, 2015:
https://www.whitehouse.gov/the-press-office/2015/04/01/executive-order-blocking -property-certain-persons-engaging-significant-m

"Obama Raises Spectre of Future Cyber War Ahead of Xi Jinping's Visit, Promises That China Cannot Win," *South China Morning Post*, September 12, 2015. As of December 1, 2015:
http://www.scmp.com/news/world/article/1857499/obama-issues-tough-warning- china-against-cyber-attacks-ahead-xi-jinpings?page=all

"Official Urges China-U.S. Trust on Cyber Security," Xinhua, April 10, 2013. As of December 2, 2015:
http://www.chinadaily.com.cn/china/2013-04/10/content_16388107.htm

Oh, Julia, "Cyber Cooperation in Northeast Asia: An Interview with James Lewis," National Bureau of Asian Research, Policy Q&A, March 17, 2015. As of November 30, 2015:
http://nbr.org/downloads/pdfs/psa/Lewis_interview_031715.pdf

Ostroukh, Audrey, "Russia, China Forge Closer Ties with New Economic, Financing Accords," *Wall Street Journal,* May 8, 2015. As of December 2, 2015:
http://www.wsj.com/articles/russia-china-forge-closer-ties-with-new-economic -financing-accords-1431099095

Perlez, Jane, "Strident Video by Chinese Military Casts U.S. as Menace," *New York Times*, October 31, 2013. As of November 30, 2015:
http://sinosphere.blogs.nytimes.com/2013/10/31/strident-video-by-chinese-military -casts-u-s-as-menace/?_r=0

Perlroth, Nicole, "Nissan Is Latest Company to Get Hacked," *New York Times*, April 24, 2012. As of December 2, 2015:
http://bits.blogs.nytimes.com/2012/04/24/nissan-is-latest-company-to-get-hacked/ ?_r=0

———, "Hackers in China Attacked the *Times* for Last Four Months," *New York Times*, January 31, 2013. As of December 2, 2015:
http://www.nytimes.com/2013/01/31/technology/chinese-hackers-infiltrate -new-york-times-computers.html

———, "China Is Said to Use Powerful New Weapon to Censor the Internet," *New York Times*, April 10, 2015. As of December 1, 2015: http://www.nytimes.com/2015/04/11/technology/china-is-said-to-use-powerful -new-weapon-to-censor-internet.html?_r=0

Qian Yingyi, Jia Qingguo, Bai Chong'en, and Wang Jisi, "Building Mutual Trust Between China and the U.S.," in Shao Binhong, ed., *The World in 2020 According to China: Chinese Foreign Policy Elites Discuss Emerging Trends in International Politics*, Leiden, The Netherlands: Koninklijke Brill NV, 2014, pp. 277–291.

Rauscher, Karl Frederick, and Zhou Yonglin, *Fighting Spam to Build Trust*, New York: EastWest Institute, 2011. As of November 30, 2015: http://www.eastwest.ngo/sites/default/files/ideas-files/China-US-Fighting -Spam.pdf

Riley, Michael A., and Sophia Pearson, "China-Based Hackers Target Law Firms to Get Secret Deal Data," Bloomberg, January 31, 2012. As of December 2, 2015: http://www.bloomberg.com/news/articles/2012-01-31/china-based-hackers-target -law-firms

Sanger, David E., "U.S. and China Seek Arms Deal for Cyberspace," *New York Times*, September 19, 2015. As of December 2, 2015: http://www.nytimes.com/2015/09/20/world/asia/us-and-china-seek-arms -deal-for-cyberspace.html

Sanger, David E., and Martin Fackler, "N.S.A. Breached North Korean Networks Before Sony Attacks, Officials Say," *New York Times*, January 18, 2015. As of December 2, 2015: http://www.nytimes.com/2015/01/19/world/asia/nsa-tapped-into-north-korean -networks-before-sony-attack-officials-say.html

Sasso, Brendan, "Report: China Hacked Obama, McCain Campaigns in 2008," *The Hill*, June 7, 2013. As of December 2, 2015: http://thehill.com/policy/technology/304111-report-china-hacked-obama-mccain -campaigns

Schmidt, Michael S., and David E. Sanger, "5 in China Army Face U.S. Charges of Cyberattacks," *New York Times*, May 19, 2014. As of November 30, 2015: http://www.nytimes.com/2014/05/20/us/us-to-charge-chinese-workers-with -cyberspying.html

Schwartz, Matthew J., "Lockheed Martin Suffers Massive Cyberattack," *InformationWeek Dark Reading*, May 30, 2011. As of December 2, 2015: http://www.darkreading.com/risk-management/lockheed-martin-suffers-massive -cyberattack/d/d-id/1098013?

Sefton, Eliot, "Chinese 'Hacked French Ministry for G20 Data,'" *The Week*, March 8, 2011. As of December 2, 2015: http://www.theweek.co.uk/technology/7229/chinese-%E2%80%98hacked -french-ministry-g20-data%E2%80%99

Segal, Adam, "Chinese Responses to the International Strategy for Cyberspace," Council on Foreign Relations, May 23, 2011. As of December 2, 2015: http://blogs.cfr.org/asia/2011/05/23/chinese-responses-to-the-international -strategy-for-cyberspace

Shambaugh, David, "Coping with a Conflicted China," *Washington Quarterly*, Vol. 34, No. 1, winter 2011, pp. 7–27.

———, "In a Fundamental Shift, China and the US Are Now Engaged in All-Out Competition," *South China Morning Post*, June 14, 2015. As of November 30, 2015: http://www.scmp.com/comment/insight-opinion/article/1819980/fundamental -shift-china-and-us-are-now-engaged-all-out?page=all

Shen Yi, "Responding to the Challenge of the 'Offensive Internet Freedom Strategy': Analyzing Sino-US Competition and Cooperation in Global Cyberspace" ["Yingdui jingongxing hulianwang ziyou zhanlüe de tiaozhan: Xi Zhong-Mei zai quanqiu xinxi kongjian de jingzheng yu hezuo"], *World Economics and Politics* [*Shijie jingji yu zhengzhi*], No. 2, 2012, pp. 69–79.

Swaine, Michael D., "Chinese Views of Cybersecurity in Foreign Relations," *China Leadership Monitor*, No. 42, fall 2013. As of December 1, 2015: http://carnegieendowment.org/files/CLM42MS.pdf

Taylor, Rob, "Australian Spy HQ Plans Stolen by Chinese Hackers: Report," Reuters, May 27, 2013. As of December 2, 2015: http://www.reuters.com/article/2013/05/28/us-australia-hacking-idUSBRE94R02 A20130528#843ZBaqbOaYt0CzQ.97

Tejada, Carlos, "Microsoft, the 'Guardian Warriors' and China's Cybersecurity Fears," *Wall Street Journal*, July 29, 2014. As of December 1, 2015: http://blogs.wsj.com/digits/2014/07/29/microsoft-the-guardian-warriors-and -chinas-cybersecurity-fears

Thornburgh, Nathan, "Inside the Chinese Hack Attack," *Time*, August 25, 2005. As of December 2, 2015: http://content.time.com/time/nation/article/0,8599,1098371,00.html

Tiezzi, Shannon, "Taiwan Complains of 'Severe' Cyber Attacks from China," *The Diplomat*, August 15, 2014. As of December 2, 2015: http://thediplomat.com/2014/08/taiwan-complains-of-severe-cyber-attacks -from-china

———, "U.S., China Open New High-Level Cyber Talks," *The Diplomat*, December 2, 2015. As of December 21, 2015: http://thediplomat.com/2015/12/us-china-open-new-high-level-cyber-talks

"Twelve Chinese Hacker Groups Responsible for Attacks on U.S.," Homeland Security News Wire, December 16, 2011. As of December 2, 2015: http://www.homelandsecuritynewswire.com /dr20111216-twelve-chinese-hacker-groups-responsible-for-attacks-on-u-s

UN General Assembly (70th session), "Group of Governmental Experts on Developments in the Field of Information and Telecommunications in the Context of International Security," July 22, 2015. As of December 2, 2015: https://disarmament-library.un.org/UNODA/Library.nsf/93a4b64e6849591d8525 7ddc006cbf21/49ef2dd67a02448b85257ea0006d13dd/$FILE/A%2070 %20174%20GGE%20on%20Information%20&%20Telecomms%20in%20 the%20field%20of%20International%20Security.pdf

U.S. Department of Defense, *The Department of Defense Cyber Strategy*, April 2015. As of December 2, 2015: http://www.defense.gov/Portals/1/features/2015/0415_cyber-strategy/Final_2015 _DoD_CYBER_STRATEGY_for_web.pdf

U.S. Department of Homeland Security, "Cyber Storm: Securing Cyberspace," Web page, December 1, 2015. As of December 2, 2015: http://www.dhs.gov/cyber-storm-securing-cyber-space

U.S. Department of Justice, Office of Public Affairs, "U.S. Charges Five Chinese Military Hackers for Cyber Espionage Against U.S. Corporations and a Labor Organization for Commercial Advantage," Washington, D.C., May 19, 2014. As of December 2, 2015: http://www.justice.gov/opa/pr/us-charges-five-chinese-military-hackers-cyber -espionage-against-us-corporations-and-labor

Wang Xu, "China 'Open to' Cybersecurity Teamwork," *China Daily*, September 18, 2015. As of November 30, 2015: http://europe.chinadaily.com.cn/china/2015-09/18/content_21912724.htm

Wee, Sui-Lee, "China Orders Lawyers to Swear Allegiance to the Communist Party," Reuters, March 21, 2012. As of December 2, 2015: http://www.reuters.com/article/2012/03/21/us-china-lawyers-idUSBRE82K0G320 120321#MKvsxt7iv05FtiVj.97

Welch, Dylan, "Chinese Hackers 'Breach Australian Media Organizations' Ahead of G20," Australian Broadcasting Corporation, November 13, 2014. As of December 2, 2015: http://www.abc.net.au/news/2014-11-13/g20-china-affiliated-hackers-breaches -australian-media/5889442

White House, *International Strategy for Cyberspace: Prosperity, Security, and Openness in a Networked World*, Washington, D.C., May 2011, p. 10.

———, "Fact Sheet: President Xi Jinping's State Visit to the United States," Washington, D.C., September 25, 2015. As of December 2, 2015: https://www.whitehouse.gov/the-press-office/2015/09/25/fact-sheet-president -xi-jinpings-state-visit-united-states

Winterbottom, Vaughan, "In China, Constitutionalism Is a Dirty Word," *The Interpreter*, January 28, 2014. As of December 1, 2015: http://www.lowyinterpreter.org/post/2014/01/28/In-China-constitutionalism-is -a-dirty-word.aspx

Wolf, David, "Why Buy the Hardware When China Is Getting the IP for Free?" *Foreign Policy*, April 24, 2015. As of December 2, 2015: http://foreignpolicy.com/2015/04/24/ibm-technology-transfer-china-virginia -rometty-strategy-lenovo-huawei-it

Wong, Edward, "Chinese Colonel's Hard-Line Views Seep into the Mainstream," *New York Times*, October 3, 2015. As of November 30, 2015: http://www.nytimes.com/2015/10/03/world/asia/chinese-colonels-hard-line -views-seep-into-the-mainstream.html

Yadron, Danny, James T. Areddy, and Paul Mozur, "Chinese Hacking Is Deep and Diverse, Experts Say," *Wall Street Journal*, May 29, 2014. As of December 2, 2015: http://www.wsj.com/articles/china-hacking-is-deep-and-diverse-experts-say -1401408979

Yang Jian, "The Nature of the Contextual Contradictions in America's Use of the Phrase 'Cyberspace Global Commons' [Meiguo 'Wangluo kongjian quanqiu gongyu shuo' de yujing maodun jiqi benzhi]," *International Survey* [*Guoji guancha*], No. 1, 2013, pp. 46–52.

Yi Wenli, "Divergence Between China and the U.S. and the Path Toward Cooperation in Cyberspace" ["Zhong-Mei zai Wangluo Kongjian de Fenqi yu Hezuo Lujing"], *Contemporary International Relations* [*Xiandai Guoji Guanxi*], Vol. 22, No. 4, July/August 2012, pp. 124–141.

Yui, Monami, and Shingo Kawamoto, "Chinese Criminals Blamed for Record Japan Bank Cybertheft," Bloomberg, December 17, 2014. As of December 2, 2015: http://www.bloomberg.com/news/articles/2014-12-17/chinese-criminals-blamed -for-record-japan-bank-cybertheft

Zhi Linfei, "Commentary: U.S. Should Think Twice Before Retaliating Against China over Unfounded Hacking Charges," Xinhua, August 3, 2015. As of December 1, 2015: http://www.china.org.cn/world/Off_the_Wire/2015-08/03/content_36211902.htm

Zhou Wa, "Internet Regulation a Sovereign Issue: FM," *China Daily*, May 20, 2011. As of December 2, 2015: http://www.chinadaily.com.cn/china/2011-05/20/content_12545488.htm

Zhu Junqing, "Commentary: U.S. Wronging of China for Cyber Breaches Harm Mutual Trust," Xinhua, June 6, 2015.